Praise for ***Mast***
By A.C.

Colleen Flynn VINE VOICE

Short and concise guide to get you started

Reviewed in the United States on April 30, 2023

I read this book in a few hours and got started on Midjourney right away. I was able to create great images by using the tool recommended by this book. It also shows you how to create your own Discord server so your images don't get "lost" in all of the threads. There's so much information out there but this book gives you the basics to get you started in no time at all.

WendyW

Very useful

Reviewed in Canada on May 3, 2023

Verified Purchase

I was already working on Midjourney and needed something to take me to the next level. This book was very useful. So much to learn, but a wonderful app for creating book covers.

Joshua Grant

Great ways for everyday people to make incredible art!

Reviewed in the United States on March 16, 2023

A.C. Hamilton guides us through a whole new way to create fantastic art and cover images with Mastering Midjourney! We are currently living through the Artificial Intelligence (AI) revolution with brand new tools that allow the average person to create professional works of art. Hamilton hones in on one of those tools, Midjourney, in this very easy-to-use guide. As someone who uses Dalle-2 (another AI art generator) it was really interesting to follow Hamilton's guide in art creation! I really appreciated how Hamilton walked me through every step from creating an account to making some incredible pictures, and how they did this through very understandable and easy steps, all with nice sections, lists, and picture examples! Discovering Midjourney through Hamilton, I've found it to be a fantastic tool for creative professionals and everyday people looking for a bit of fun alike. If you're looking for new ways to make covers for your books, or you're just bored and want to have a bit of fun making art, definitely come check out Hamilton's guide and get on your way to Mastering Midjourney!

Mastering Midjourney
Tips & Techniques For Generating Exceptional AI Art

by A.C. Hamilton

https://digitalagemedia.net (coming soon)

Interior design by A.C. Hamilton
Cover design by A.C. Hamilton
Cover illustration by A.C. Hamilton
Interior illustrations by A.C. Hamilton
Author image by A.C. Hamilton

United States of America

V.2.2 - May 25, 2023
ISBN (Paperback): 978-1-64786-092-9
ASIN (KDP): B0BR26Q78P

COPYRIGHT & DISCLAIMER

The publisher publishes in a variety of print and electronic formats and by print-on-demand. Where applicable, some material included with standard print versions of a book may not be included in eBooks or in print-on-demand, and vice versa. Additionally, electronic versions may be subject to formatting issues on certain devices which are not within the control of the publisher. The publisher makes every effort to ensure that the content is presented in the best possible format, but some issues may arise due to limitations of the technology used by the provider.

Library of Congress Cataloging-in-Publication Data:

Names: Hamilton, A.C., author.
Title: Mastering Midjourney: Tips & Techniques For Generating Exceptional AI Art / A.C. Hamilton.
Description: Ohio : Digital Age Media, [2023] | Includes bibliographical references.
Identifiers:
LCCN 2023901334 (print) | ISBN 978-1-64786-092-9 (print)

TABLE OF CONTENTS

Foreword

The rise of AI technology has been one of the most exciting and transformative developments of recent times. In late 2022, Chat GPT was released and quickly became one of the most talked-about AI tools on the internet. As someone who has always been interested in cutting-edge technology, I was eager to explore the potential of Chat GPT and other AI tools.

Using Chat GPT, I created the first book in this AI Series, *Introduction to Chat GPT.* My goal was to raise awareness about AI technology and its many applications in everyday life. I also wanted to demonstrate the power and utility of Chat GPT by using it to create most of the first version of text for that book in just a few hours. The response to the book was overwhelmingly positive, and it inspired me to continue exploring the possibilities of AI tools.

Since then, I've kept a close eye on new advancements in AI technology and discovered Midjourney and other AI art tools. I've been amazed at how these tools can help us unlock our creativity and push the boundaries of what's possible. With *Mastering Midjourney,* it's my hope that this book will inspire readers to push their own creative boundaries and explore the possibilities of AI technology.

Lastly, once you've finished this book, please consider leaving a book review on Amazon, as I read each review personally in order to make improvements for the benefit of readers and to increase the overall value of the material, or to learn of any positive effects it's had on your journey as well. When you leave a review on Amazon, it will also help others find this book more easily in search results, so even if you don't feel like writing a long review, you can simply tap the stars ☆☆☆☆☆ you consider appropriate, and that will still help.

Thank you for putting your faith in me to learn more about artificial intelligence and Midjourney. I am confident that this book will expand your understanding of the subject and provide you with actionable insights to help you take advantage of AI technology.

A.C.

Introduction

As someone who has spent countless hours exploring the world of AI-generated art, Midjourney is one of the most best platforms available in terms of quality and versatility. In this guide, I want to share my insights and knowledge to help you unleash the full potential of this amazing tool.

With the power of AI, artists can create works that were previously impossible, incorporating the styles of specific artists into their own work, easily generating images of different environments, and making use of high resolutions and post-production techniques. The possibilities are endless, and as the technology continues to evolve, we're only scratching the surface of what's to come.

How Does Midjourney Work?

Midjourney is an AI-powered tool that creates images using Diffusion models. Diffusion models are a type of generative model that can create new data similar to the data they were trained on. They add noise to the training data and then learn how to remove it to recover the original data. Once trained, the Diffusion model can generate new data by passing random noise through the learned denoising process, making it possible to create images from noise.

In simpler terms, Diffusion models gradually transform data into pure Gaussian noise, a type of statistical noise that follows a normal distribution. Gaussian noise is often added to data and image processing to simulate random errors or disturbances that can occur in real-world situations. The goal of training the model is to learn how to reverse this process, allowing new data to be generated. This can be useful for creating unique images or other types of data.

During the training phase, the AI distorts the original image with noise until it is almost unrecognizable, and then learns how to recover the original image from the noisy version. This process is repeated many times, resulting in a model that can generate images from random noise and a prompt.

One of the most exciting features of Midjourney is the randomness of the generated images. Even if the same prompt is entered multiple times, the images generated will always be different. This is because Midjourney incorporates elements from a vast array of images during the training phase, allowing the AI to create unique images based on the user's input.

The AI's ability to generate completely unique images means that artists can create pieces that are truly one-of-a-kind. Additionally, the wide variety of channels available on the Midjourney Discord server, including rooms for newbies, show and tell, and paint overs, make it easy for artists to connect with others and get inspired by the work of their peers.

When using Midjourney, the generated images may not always be what you expect, especially when using common subjects like trees. If you prompt Midjourney with just "tree," the generated images may be highly-stylized or abstract interpretations of a tree, rather than a photorealistic image.

To get closer to a photo-realistic image of a tree, you should be more specific with your prompt. For example, try using prompts like "an oak tree with leaves in the autumn, photorealistic" or just "a pine tree with snow on the branches." This will give Midjourney more specific details to work with, resulting in a more realistic image that still retains some of the stylized or artistic elements that make Midjourney unique.

Part of the fun of using Midjourney is seeing how the AI interprets your prompt and generates an image. The more familiar you become with prompts, parameters, and the results, you'll learn how to adapt prompts to hone in on the results you want. Don't be afraid to experiment and see what kind of unique and creative images you can come up with.

That being said, it's important to remember that Midjourney is only as good as the prompts you provide. It's important to keep this in mind and be prepared for not every image to turn out as expected. However, with patience and experimentation, you can learn to create exceptional AI-generated artwork that reflects your unique vision.

You're going to need a basic understanding of Discord and how to navigate the platform in order to use Midjourney, so I'll be covering each relevant aspect as the book progresses to equip you with direct information to make the process seamless.

Midjourney furnishes a number of exciting features for image generation. It allows you to incorporate influence and style to guide the image generation process and create works that truly reflect your vision. Using descriptive text prompts and reference images and weights, you can fine-tune the image generation process to better align with your vision. Additionally, Midjourney offers a range of render engine styles to choose from, allowing you to select the best style for your image. This book explore these features and provide examples of successful images created using each one.

By becoming familiar with these newer features and advances in Midjourney, you'll be equipped with the tools and knowledge you need to create exceptional AI-generated artwork. It's important to note that Midjourney is constantly evolving, with new tools and features being added all the time. As you become more experienced with the platform, you can experiment with these new features and push the boundaries of what's possible with AI art.

I'll also provide you with useful references, resources, and commands that you can use to create exceptional AI-generated artwork with Midjourney throughout the book. With this guide, you'll be able to unlock the full potential of Midjourney and create stunning art that is truly unique and original.

CHAPTER 1: MIDJOURNEY COPYRIGHT & COMMERCIAL USE

Before you start using Midjourney, you should know exactly what you can do with the art you create. It's important to understand the philosophy behind the company's product before we get into the specifics of how Midjourney's copyright and trademark terms work as well.

Midjourney's goal is to create a collaborative space where everyone can create various pieces of art that can be shared with the community. In other words, Midjourney encourages the sharing and recycling of other users' Midjourney images because it helps the AI improve over time.

The vast majority of users' images are publicly visible to all and can be re-used to create new images by anyone. Once you understand this philosophy, you won't be surprised to learn that Midjourney's server terms essentially state the following:

Midjourney's Rights:

- Perpetual, non-exclusive, and worldwide rights.
- The right to sublicense, reproduce and prepare derivative works.
- Rights to publicly display, perform, and distribute images and text prompts.

Your Rights:

- You "own" all the assets created with Midjourney.
- However, they can still be used and remixed by others.
- You can use the images commercially, provided you are a paid user.

If this appears confusing, it essentially states that everything you create with Midjourney can be used by Midjourney as well as anyone else. And different levels of usage rights are granted depending on whether you are a free or paying user.

Rights of Non-Paid Users

Non-paying users are granted an asset license under the Creative Commons Noncommercial 4.0 Attribution license under the Midjourney copyright terms. That is, you are free to do whatever you want with the images as long as it is not for commercial purposes. Furthermore, Midjourney must be acknowledged.

Rights of Paid Users

The rules for paid users are fairly straightforward. You can basically do whatever you want with the images you create. The only exception is if you created the images for a company with a yearly revenue of more than $1 million. If you fall into that category, you must join Midjourney's corporate membership.

What Does Commercial Use Mean?

Commercial use in the context of Midjourney means that you can use it for business purposes, as long as you do not fall into the "corporate" category.

Business purposes include, but are not limited to:

- Marketing material

- Posters
- Book covers
- Album covers
- Printed apparel
- Merchandise

I'm cautious to list NFTs here because the AI and blockchain scenes are still very new, and many legal questions have yet to be answered.

Technically, one could argue that the NFT is the blockchain entry, while the artwork is part of the visual identity and marketing.

In that case, using Midjourney artwork for NFTs is permissible; nevertheless, it makes it impossible to legally prevent someone else from using the same artwork.

Copyright Works Differently Around The World

As a sidebar, I'd like to point out that the way copyright is commonly handled in the United States differs significantly from that of other jurisdictions.

Transferring copyright to someone is quite usual, at least figuratively. That is not conceivable in many European countries because the copyright always belongs to the original inventor in perpetuity. Instead, you can sell or transfer the rights to a work. This is especially relevant in the context of AI artwork, because it is uncertain whether the AI should be considered an "artist" or not.

As a sidebar, I'd like to point out that the way copyright is commonly handled in the United States differs significantly from that of other jurisdictions.

Frequently Asked Questions (FAQ)

Before I wrap up this section I will address some of the most frequently asked questions about Midjourney copyright and commercial use.

Can I use Midjourney commercially?

Yes, if you are a paying member, you may use Midjourney photos for commercial purposes. It can be used as marketing material, cover art, or even printed on items and sold.

Is Midjourney royalty-free?

Midjourney-created images are royalty-free. That is, your membership price effectively pays for your usage privileges. No extra costs or royalties are payable after you use the artwork, regardless of how frequently or how much you charge for it.

Are Midjourney images free to use?

The Midjourney copyright terms provide you a Creative Commons Noncommercial 4.0 license if you are a non-paid user. This implies that you must provide clear attribution whenever you utilize the artwork.

Who owns the copyright on Midjourney text prompts?

Experts in copyright law are still divided on whether text prompts have a sufficient "creative level" to be considered for copyright, especially given how brief and generic they are. However, the Midjourney terms of service make it plain that by entering them into the tool, you are basically providing everyone the right to use them as well. As a result, the answer is relatively irrelevant.

How to Buy And Cancel Your Midjourney Subscription

This quick section will help you navigate the process of purchasing and canceling a Midjourney subscription with ease. Whether you're new to Midjourney or have been using the service for a while, this guide will provide you with all the information you need to know.

Buying a Midjourney Subscription

If you've already created a trial account and want to become a paid member of Midjourney, the first step is to access your account page on the Midjourney website. There are two ways to get to the account page:

- **Method 1:** Navigate to your Account at the URL below using your browser.
  https://www.midjourney.com/account/

- **Method 2:** Type the **/subscribe** command inside the Midjourney Discord and click the "Open subscription page" button.

Regardless of which method you choose, the interface looks the same, so you'll have no trouble finding what you need. Once you're on the account page, simply click on the "Subscribe" button to choose the membership plan you want.

Midjourney Subscription Plans:

Midjourney offers four different membership plans to choose from: Basic, Standard, Pro, and Corporate. Each plan comes with different benefits and pricing, so be sure to select the plan that best suits your needs.

Here's a rundown of the different membership plans available on Midjourney:

- **Basic Membership:**
    - Price: $10/month
    - Jobs: 200/month
    - No access to relax mode
    - Upgrade receive proportional discounts
    - Private visibility available at a $20 surcharge
- **Standard Membership:**
    - Price: $30/month
    - Jobs: Unlimited (technically ~ 900)
    - Access to Midjourney's relax mode
    - Upgrade receive proportional discounts
    - Private visibility available at a $20 surcharge
- **Pro Membership:**
    - Price: $60/month
    - Jobs: Unlimited (technically ~ 1800)
    - Access to Midjourney's relax mode
    - Upgrade receive proportional discounts
    - Free private visibility
- **Corporate Membership (phaseout not confirmed yet):**
    - Price: $600/year
    - Jobs: Unlimited (technically ~7,200)
    - Everything else like the Standard Membership
    - Free private visibility
    - This plan is compulsory for employees of companies that make more than $1 million in revenue per year.

After selecting your preferred membership plan, you'll be taken to Midjourney's checkout page, which is hosted by Stripe. Enter your payment details and click the "Subscribe" button one more time to complete the process.

Canceling Your Midjourney Subscription

Canceling your Midjourney subscription is just as easy as becoming a paid member. If you need to cancel your subscription, follow these simple steps:

- **Method 1:** Navigate to your Account at the URL below using your browser. https://www.midjourney.com/account/
- **Method 2:** Type the **/subscribe** command inside the Midjourney Discord and click the "Open subscription page" button.

Once you're on the subscription page, look for the "Manage subscription" button or link, and click it. You may be asked to confirm your decision to cancel your plan. Once you've confirmed, your plan will be canceled, and it will not renew once the billing cycle has ended.

It's important to note that canceling your subscription will not restrict your account until the full billing cycle has ended. This means that even if you cancel your subscription immediately after signing up, you'll still have access to the full benefits of a paid membership until the end of the billing cycle.

Frequently Asked Questions (FAQ)

Here are some of the most commonly asked questions related to Midjourney subscriptions:

Does the Midjourney subscription automatically renew every month?

Yes, Midjourney subscriptions always renew automatically. Your credit card will be billed on a recurring basis unless you actively cancel your subscription. It's important to note that deleting your Discord account is not enough to cancel your Midjourney subscription, as they are completely separate.

Why can't I cancel my Midjourney subscription?

If your credit card was declined after a recent membership renewal, you will not be able to cancel your subscription until you pay the amount that is still due.

Why don't I see any option to cancel on the Midjourney account page?

Make sure that you have logged in with the correct Discord account. Your subscription is linked to the Discord account that you used when you subscribed. If you have logged into a different account, then the website has no way of knowing who you are.

Can I un-cancel my Midjourney subscription if I change my mind?

Yes, even if you have canceled your membership, you can still "un-cancel" or "reactivate" it as long as the billing cycle hasn't ended. Simply follow the same process outlined in the previous section to access the subscription page and reactivate your plan.

Summary

Copyright and trademark regulations have always been a source of concern, and with the arrival of artificial intelligence, the situation is only worsening. Some individuals may be confused by the Midjourney copyright conditions, but as long as you're a paying member, you have nothing to worry about and can do whatever you want. It's also vital to remember that, even though you're the “owner,” you're indirectly granting any other user the ability to remix and use the photos you generate.

CHAPTER 2: DISCOVERING DISCORD

Discord is an adaptable social platform that has transformed from a chat software for gamers to a comprehensive communication tool that provides a multitude of features such as text, voice, and video chat. As the hub for connecting with similar individuals, engaging in lively discussions, and participating in various activities with apps that have integrated Discord into their functionality, Discord is a critical component of the Midjourney experience. To use Midjourney efficiently, mastering Discord's navigation is essential.

Discord started as a simple chat software for gamers and has grown into a full-fledged social platform that offers texting, voice, and video calls to connect with friends or strangers who share common interests. It's like Zoom, but more flexible and fun. It's Slack, but without the pressure of feeling like your boss is always lurking. Facebook, without the algorithms that prioritize posts that turned your aunt into a racist. Twitter, without the whims of a mercurial overlord. In short, it's different, and it's worth exploring.

Getting Started With Discord

To get started with Discord, you can use it on your mobile device or desktop computer. There are mobile apps available for both Android and iOS devices. On a computer, you can use it in your web browser if you want to keep it simple, or download the desktop client to access more advanced features such as game overlays. The desktop client is available for Windows, MacOS, and Linux.

Here are some steps to help you get started with Discord, so you can use it to navigate Midjourney with ease:

- **Download Discord:** You can download the Discord app for free from the official website at the URL below, or through your app store on your mobile device. The app is available for Windows, MacOS, and Linux, as well as for Android and iOS mobile devices. https://discord.com/download

- **Create an account:** Once you've downloaded Discord, you'll need to create an account. To do so, enter your email and create a unique username and password. You'll need to verify your email address to complete your account setup.

- **Join the Midjourney server:** To access Midjourney, you'll need to join the server at the URL below. Servers are like forums or chat rooms where people can connect with others who share common interests. You'll receive an invitation link to the Midjourney server, which you can use to join the community and, thus, access the platform.
https://rebrand.ly/discord-midjourney-signup

- **Customize your profile:** You can customize your profile by changing your profile picture, username, and status.

To do so, click on the user settings and make the desired changes.

By following these steps, you can begin learning to navigate Discord, which will help you use Midjourney more efficiently. Discord is a popular tool for communication, networking, and collaboration, so it's worth taking the time to learn how to use it.

Understanding The Discord Interface

For beginners, the Discord interface can be overwhelming. There are four main sections on the main Discord interface. On the far left side of your screen, you'll see the servers you're a part of, each with its own icon. When you tap the name of a server, the screen will change, and you'll see a list of channels on the right. These channels are the chat rooms within the server, and each channel is about a specific topic. Channels are separated into multiple dropdown menus called categories. To switch to a different topic, click on a different channel.

To the right of the main chat panel is a list of all the users on that server. You can see who is online and what their activity level is. Swipe from side to side to switch between all the panels on mobile. Click or tap the top left blue Discord logo to see your list of friends as well as any direct messages you've received.

Communicating on Discord

Discord has two main ways to communicate: text and voice. Text channels have a hashtag (#) symbol in front of them, and these are the channels where you go for typing. When the name of a channel is in bold font, that means there are unread messages in the chat. To reply to a comment or react with an emoji, select the message and look for the buttons to the right of the text. You can also start a thread, which nests more comments below the one you've selected. It's a way to digress on a topic without cluttering up the rest of the channel feed.

On the other hand, voice channels are usually located down toward the bottom of the channel panel. They're marked with a little speaker icon. If you click or tap on one of those voice channels, you'll be instantly connected to the voice chat. Depending on the server's settings, everybody in the channel might suddenly be privy to your heavy breathing. To avoid this, down by your profile name, there's a mic button. Tap that to mute yourself. It'll stay muted even when you join new sessions.

On the desktop, there's an indicator down in the lower left corner—just above your username—that says Voice Connected. It means what you think it does. On mobile, there will be a persistent green band at the top of your screen letting you know your audio is connected. To disconnect from the channel, tap Voice Connected and hit the end call button. If the server allows it, you can also toggle on your camera for a video chat. The active video screens will pop up in the main panel.

To ensure that you don't embarrass yourself on Discord, check your privacy settings. Discord enables a lot of data collection at the start, and you'll want to control what everyone can find out about you. Tap or click the little gear icon by your username (User Settings) and go into Privacy & Safety. There, you can tell Discord to filter NSFW messages and servers, decide whether to let strangers message you, and control the types of activity data you send back to Discord.

Discord will also display some of your activity by default. If you're playing a game on your computer, for example, Discord automatically shows what you're playing to everyone who can see your status. That means all your friends and anyone in a public server. To control that visibility, tap your profile pic. You'll be able to choose a status there, either Online, Idle, Do Not Disturb, or Invisible. If you want to appear offline and hide your activity, select Invisible. As an extra precaution, you can go into your User Settings, then go down to Activity Settings. Uncheck "Display current activity as a status message." That will keep your activity out of your status even if you're set to Online.

Lastly, it's important to know the etiquette of the server you're in. Some servers may require you to read the rules before you can start posting. Every group has different policies, and if you're joining an existing group, you'll want to take some time to figure out what is and isn't allowed.

Finding Communities on Discord

One of the great things about Discord is that there are a ton of communities to join, some massive and some tiny. The more obscure ones may require invites from people already in the server. Substacks, Patreon creators, or Kickstarter campaigns offer access to private Discord servers as rewards for paying backers.

To find communities, you can use the Explore Public Servers option at the bottom of the servers panel. Open that up, and you'll find some of the top servers across Discord. The big categories are Gaming, Music, Education, Science and Tech, and Entertainment. If you're in school, Student Hubs can help you find groups and clubs with your classmates.

You can also use Discord to network and make professional connections. Many businesses have servers for their employees, and you can also find servers for specific industries. If you're a freelancer, you can find other freelancers to collaborate with or even find work.

Premium Features and Customizations

While the core Discord experience is free, there are also paid subscription tiers available for those who want more features and customization options. The first tier is Nitro Basic, which costs less than half the price of Nitro and offers a slimmer selection of premium goodies. With Nitro Basic, users get access to larger file uploads, animated profile pictures, and custom emojis. The second tier is Nitro, which costs $10 per month or $100 a year. With Nitro, users get all the features of Nitro Basic, as well as the ability to set up multiple profiles, have profile banners, and access to a larger selection of custom stickers.

In addition to the Nitro tiers, users can also choose to "boost" a server, which gives the community some benefits that everyone can use. This can mean more emoji, higher audio and video streaming quality, and the ability to upload bigger files. The more users that boost, the more premiums unlock for the entire community.

Finally, users can customize their servers with their own personal touch. This includes creating custom roles, setting up moderation permissions, and creating their own channels. Additionally, users can add bots to their servers to help with moderation or to add fun features like music playback or games. There are countless ways to customize and enhance the Discord experience, and the platform encourages users to experiment and make it their own.

With a little bit of exploration and experimentation, you can create your own personalized Discord experience that suits your interests and needs.

Summary

Discord is a powerful social platform that provides a wide range of features for communication, collaboration, and networking. It's an essential part of the Midjourney experience, providing a central hub for connecting with other like-minded individuals and creating digital art. By mastering Discord's navigation, you'll be able to use Midjourney more efficiently and take full advantage of its AI art platform capabilities.

In the next chapter, I will go over the different versions of Midjourney and discuss the features of the latest version (V5).

Chapter 3: Midjourney Versions

In order to fully appreciate and understand how to use the latest iteration of Midjourney, which is Version 5 (V5), it's important to understand the chronology of the previous versions. So, before diving into the specifics of using Midjourney V5, let's take a look at the evolution of the tool.

Midjourney was first released in March 2022 with limited functionality, but it generated significant interest in the potential of AI art tools. Since then, the team behind Midjourney has continued to refine and improve the tool, releasing several new versions with expanded features and capabilities. In the following sections, I'll briefly go over the history of Midjourney and explore each version's evolution leading up to the latest iteration. Don't worry if some of the references are unclear at this stage; I'll explain them more fully in later chapters. After providing this context, I'll move on to explaining how to use Midjourney.

Version 1: March 2022

The initial version of this technology was nothing short of astounding when it was first introduced. As we reflect on its development and progress over time, it's easy to dismiss the early iteration as being inadequate compared to its successors. However, it is crucial to appreciate the remarkable capabilities of Version 1 (V1) during its early days, as it laid the groundwork for future advancements.

In the V1 model, there was a notable limitation: users could not control the amount of detail added during the upscaling process. This shortcoming was addressed and rectified in subsequent versions, providing users with a greater degree of customization and precision when enhancing images or content. Regardless, it is essential to recognize and appreciate the groundbreaking achievements of V1, as it served as a catalyst for the continual improvement and refinement of the technology.

Version 2: April 2022

Version 2 marked a significant enhancement over the original iteration, as it demonstrated improvements in the coherence of compositions and the recognizability of text. Additionally, the upscaling capability was refined, allowing for the addition of more intricate details to images, ultimately resulting in higher-resolution outputs. However, images produced by this version were still somewhat gritty in appearance.

Users expressed a desire for features that would grant them more control over various parameters during the generation process, specifically to reduce grittiness, introduce softness, and create a cleaner appearance with less noise. Responding to this feedback, the Midjourney team went on to develop Version 3, which introduced the innovative Light Upscale feature.

With the implementation of Light Upscale in Version 3, users were granted more control over the image enhancement process, ultimately leading to a much-improved image quality. This new feature enabled the creation of cleaner and less noisy images, catering to the specific requests of the user base and further advancing the technology.

Version 3: July 2022

Version 3 brought about significant advancements in image quality, and with the introduction of the Light Upscale feature, users were able to generate images with fewer artifacts. Utilizing the --uplight option ensured that the AI did not overprocess the images, maintaining an appealing balance of softness and detail.

Two essential features were incorporated into the new V3 algorithms: --stylize and --quality. The --stylize parameter determined the intensity of stylization applied to the images. By increasing this value, the resulting images would exhibit a more distinctive and unique style. However, setting the parameter too high could lead the AI to become overly opinionated, potentially causing it to disregard the user's input.

On the other hand, the --quality parameter provided users with the ability to control the amount of processing time the algorithm dedicated to image generation. This parameter not only affected the overall image quality but also influenced the cost associated with image production. For example, setting the quality to 0.5 would result in images costing half the standard rate, while setting it to 2 would double the cost.

Overall, the enhancements in Version 3 offered users greater control over the image generation process, enabling the production of visually appealing images that were tailored to their specific preferences and requirements.

Version 4: November 2022

Version 4 marked a significant departure from previous iterations, as it was developed from the ground up and initially released as an Alpha version. According to an announcement shared on Midjourney's Discord, the V4 base model boasted several notable enhancements:

- A vast expansion of knowledge, encompassing creatures, places, and more
- A heightened ability to accurately capture small details in all situations
- Improved handling of complex prompts, featuring multiple levels of detail

- Enhanced performance in multi-object and multi-character scenes
- Support for advanced features such as image prompting and multi-prompts
- The addition of a --chaos parameter (ranging from 0 to 100) for controlling the diversity of image grids

The development timeline of Midjourney's models reveals that the initial versions underwent rapid iterations, followed by a more extended period before the release of Version 4. This new version represented a substantial improvement in various aspects, including realism, image cohesion, and overall aesthetics. After another extended wait, Version 5 was eventually made available, promising further enhancements and capabilities to continue pushing the boundaries of this innovative technology.

Version 5: March 2023

At present, the alpha release of Version 5 is undergoing rigorous testing and fine-tuning to optimize its performance and capabilities. As a result, the final stable release of V5 may exhibit a different default aesthetic than its current iteration. In the subsequent sections, I will delve into the various features and enhancements that have been introduced in this latest version.

Higher Native Resolution

With the introduction of Midjourney V5, images are now rendered at a significantly higher native resolution compared to its predecessor, V4. The default resolution has doubled, increasing from 512 x 512 pixels to 1024 x 1024 pixels. This enhancement eliminates the need to upscale V4 images to achieve the same resolution, representing a substantial improvement in overall image quality.

In the future, we may witness the development of V5 upscalers capable of further augmenting the resolution to dimensions such as 2048 x 2048 pixels. However, for the time being, the 1024 x 1024 pixel resolution serves as both the default and maximum output for Midjourney V5 images.

Unlimited Aspect Ratios

In contrast to its predecessor, Midjourney V5 offers a more flexible approach to aspect ratios, providing users with unlimited possibilities. Initially, when Midjourney V4 was launched, it only supported the square aspect ratio (1:1). Over time, the range of supported aspect ratios expanded, eventually accommodating 2:3 / 3:2 and ultimately reaching resolutions of up to 1:2 / 2:1.

This evolution in aspect ratio support exemplifies the ongoing development and refinement of the Midjourney platform, enabling users to generate images that cater to their specific requirements and preferences.

Sharper, More Detailed Images

The images generated by Midjourney V5 exhibit significantly enhanced sharpness and detail compared to those produced by its predecessor, V4. To illustrate this improvement, consider the following example: when given the prompt *"photo of two children tossing a baseball,"* the images created by V5 display a remarkable increase in clarity and intricacy compared to the outputs generated by V4.

This enhancement in image quality demonstrates the substantial progress made in the development of the Midjourney platform, ultimately delivering more lifelike and visually appealing results to users.

V4

V5

At first inspection, the V4 image appears to be accurate. Nevertheless, upon closer examination, this immediately fails scrutiny (zoom in to see). The children's faces are not quite photorealistic, their hands are questionable in a few images, and the baseballs could also stand some improvement. V5, however, appears to be actual photographs. The level of detail is astounding.

More Coherent Output

Midjourney V5 has also made significant strides in producing more coherent outputs, improving the overall visual composition and addressing several issues that were present in V4. Some of the notable enhancements include:

- Improved representation of large groups of people
- More accurate and realistic hands, with the correct number of fingers (in most cases)
- A reduction in random artifacts appearing in images

To demonstrate these advancements, consider the outcome of the following prompt: *"candid photo of a crowd of people at a live concert."* The images generated by V5 showcase the platform's progress in delivering visually consistent and appealing results.

V4

V5

At first glance, the images generated by both V4 and V5 may appear quite similar. However, upon closer inspection, it becomes evident that V4 images tend to exhibit twisted features and other peculiar attributes. In contrast, while not flawless, Version 5 demonstrates a considerable improvement in reducing such anomalies and excels in rendering more distinguishable facial characteristics.

Wider Range of Supported Styles

Midjourney V5 boasts a significantly broader scope of supported styles compared to its predecessor, V4. As stated by the Midjourney team, V5 offers a stylistic range that is five times greater than that of V4. In practice, this implies that with the appropriate prompts, users can generate a wide variety of styles and specialized images using Version 5.

Furthermore, Version 5 has demonstrated a particular proficiency in rendering landscapes and architectural structures. This expanded range of supported styles exemplifies the platform's ongoing advancements and its ability to cater to diverse user needs and preferences. Here's a brief example:

Skyscraper V5

Lava flowing from a volcano V5

More Nuanced Understanding of Text Prompts

Midjourney V5 also exhibits a more nuanced understanding of text prompts, thanks to advancements in natural language processing (NLP). This improvement enables users to experiment with more elaborate, descriptive suggestions in the form of complete sentences, allowing them to achieve their desired outcomes more effectively. (This is not the same as splatterprompting.)

Support for Tiling

Midjourney is reintroducing support for tiling, a feature that was initially present in Version 3 but was absent in Version 4. This functionality enables users to generate "tiles" or modular image elements that can be seamlessly interlocked to create a repeating pattern.

For instance, consider using an emoji prompt like *:partying_face:* 🥳 to initiate the tiling process. The resulting tiles can be used to form a visually engaging pattern that showcases the chosen emoji in a recurring design.

The return of tiling support highlights the platform's commitment to providing users with diverse features and options, allowing them to create unique and captivating images tailored to their needs.

Better Handling of Image Prompts (and remixes)

Midjourney Version 5 demonstrates improved performance when it comes to handling image prompts and remixes, leading to more accurate and predictable results. This enhanced capability allows users to incorporate image prompts with greater confidence, knowing that the platform can effectively interpret and process the input to generate desired outputs.

Support for Image Weights

This is yet another feature from V3 that wasn't available in V4. Well, it's returned in V5! It lets you decide how much priority Midjourney gives to the image compared to the text part of the prompt.

You assign image weights by evoking the --iw parameter, followed by a number between 0.5 (lowest weight) to 2 (highest weight). Like so:

Image weights give you a powerful way to experiment and find just the right balance between text and image input.

No Built-In Aesthetic (yet)

Midjourney's latest version, V5 alpha, has been deemed "less opinionated" by its crew. This means that the software no longer defaults to a specific "look" like its predecessor, V4, which often produced an almost-but-not-quite realistic close-up of a woman's face. Instead, V5 offers users the freedom to create their exact vision using detailed and specific prompts. However, this also means that users can no longer rely on Midjourney to generate predictable outputs with little effort.

To use an analogy, V4 was like Mr. Potato Head—able to rearrange facial features in many ways but still fundamentally the same. V5, on the other hand, is like Play Doh, allowing for complete creative control and endless possibilities.

Midjourney has assured users that the upcoming "stable" version of V5 will have its own built-in aesthetic. However, for now, users may need to learn some V5 tricks to achieve the desired result.

In the next chapter, I will provide a detailed explanation of how to use Midjourney with Discord. I will cover various parameters, tools, and features that are available, and guide you through the interface to help you create some awesome art so you can enjoy a seamless and exciting experience.

CHAPTER 4: USING MIDJOURNEY

Now that you have an understanding of using Discord and an overview of the Midjourney versions, I'll elaborate more on how to begin using Midjourney. As discussed in **Chapter 2**, the first step is to visit their website and sign up for their beta program. This will give you access to their Discord server, where you can interact with the Midjourney Bot and start creating your artwork. You can sign up for the beta program at this URL: https://rebrand.ly/discord-midjourney-signup

When you first enter the Midjourney Discord server, take your time and explore at your own pace. Hiding the member list in the top right corner can help declutter the interface, and ignoring the download button unless you want to run the bot locally is recommended. Once you are ready to start using the Bot, you will be able to begin creating your own art.

Keep in mind that as a free user, you will only have access to 10 credits or hours of usage, while paid members have more. There is a lot of information available within the Discord server, so be sure to take your time and explore those as well. https://docs.midjourney.com/docs

The key to a successful experience using Midjourney is to have fun and be inventive. Go at your own speed, pause and return when you need, and take breaks as necessary to avoid feeling anxious or overwhelmed. With time and effort, you will learn to master the Bot and be able to use it to produce amazing works of art.

The image below is an example of the type of images you can create; in this case, it was my experimentation with images I wanted to repurpose into a book cover using Canva to add custom text and other elements not available through Midjourney.

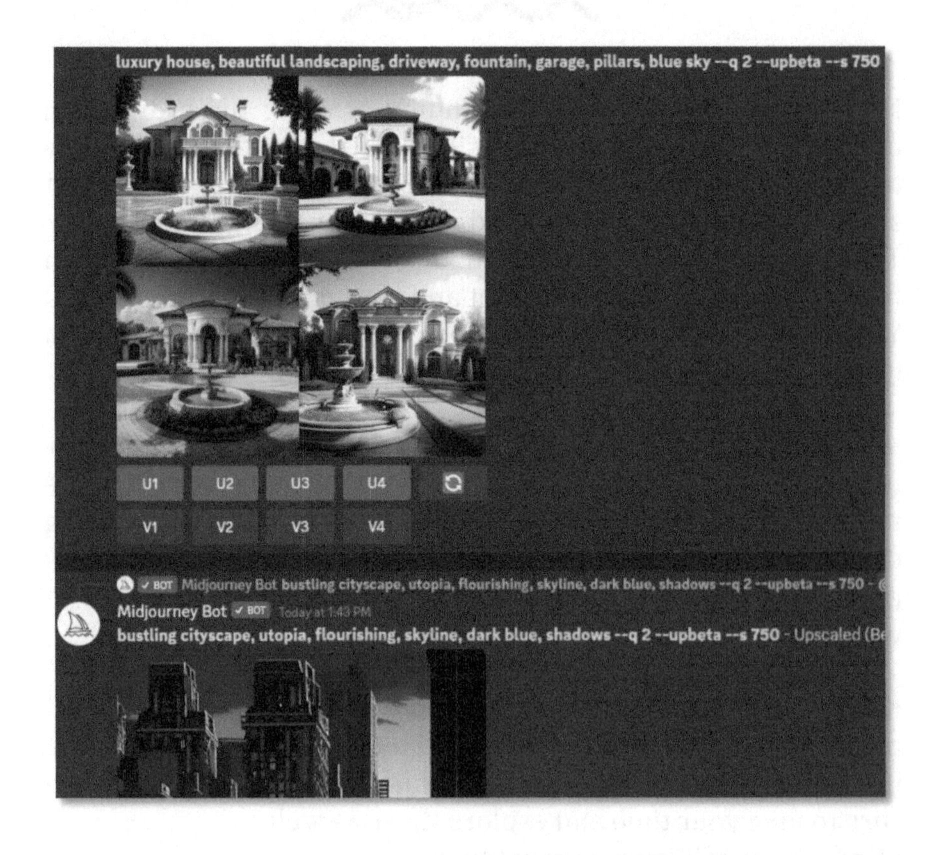

I fed Midjourney the prompt "luxury house, beautiful landscaping, driveway, fountain, garage, pillars, blue sky —q 2 —upbeta —s 750," and this is what the Bot produced as the first batch of images (you will always receive a grid of four images).

The potential for what you can accomplish with each image is vast from this point, but before exploring that, I'll explain the process of adding the Midjourney Bot to your own server, which simplifies the use of Midjourney.

How To Use The Midjourney Bot In Your Own Server

This section will show you a better way to manage your art and avoid losing track of images in a public "newbie" room. This can be done by adding the Midjourney Bot to your own Discord server. By implementing this technique, you can keep track of all your art in one place within your own Channel(s), without having to scroll up and down constantly to find your generated images. I'll be illustrating how to do this from the Midjourney mobile app, but the steps should be the same across all versions.

Here's three simple steps to add the Midjourney Bot to your Discord server:

1. Create a Server
2. Add the Midjourney Bot to your server
3. Use **/imagine** followed by keywords

Create a Server

On the left menu bar, select the **Plus** button near the bottom. At the next screen, choose **Create My Own**.

Add the Midjourney Bot to your server

Go to any newbies channel (e.g., **#newbies-117** shown in the previous image). Next, select the **Profile** icon at the top right corner. Then, select the **Midjourney Bot**.

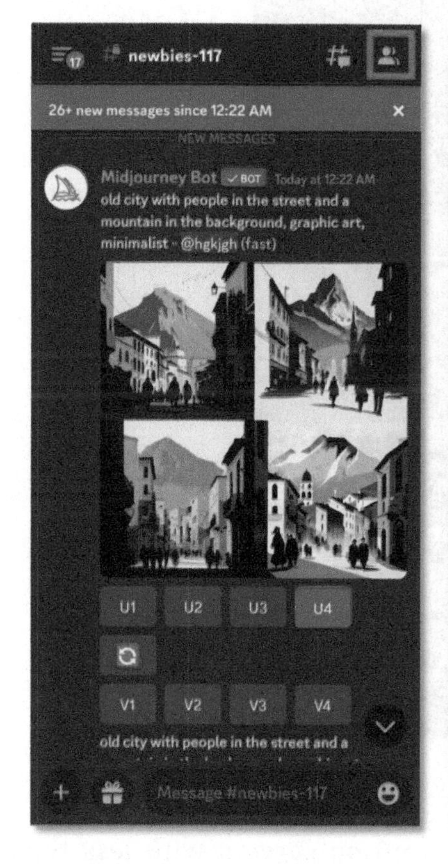

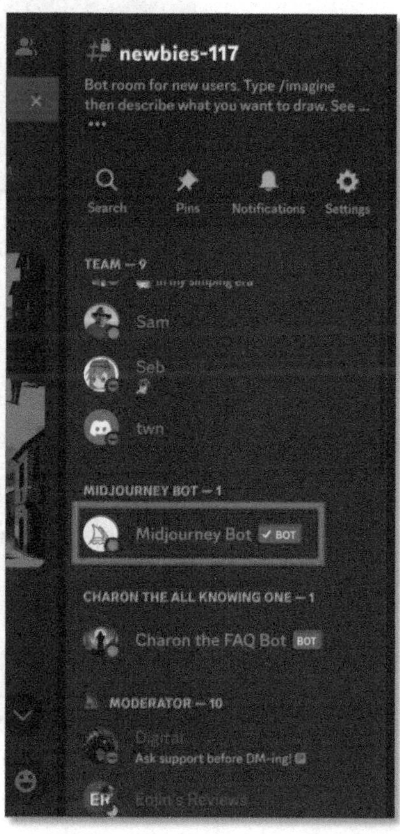

On the next screen, you'll choose **Add to Server**, and then choose the server you created and select **Continue**, then **Authorize.**

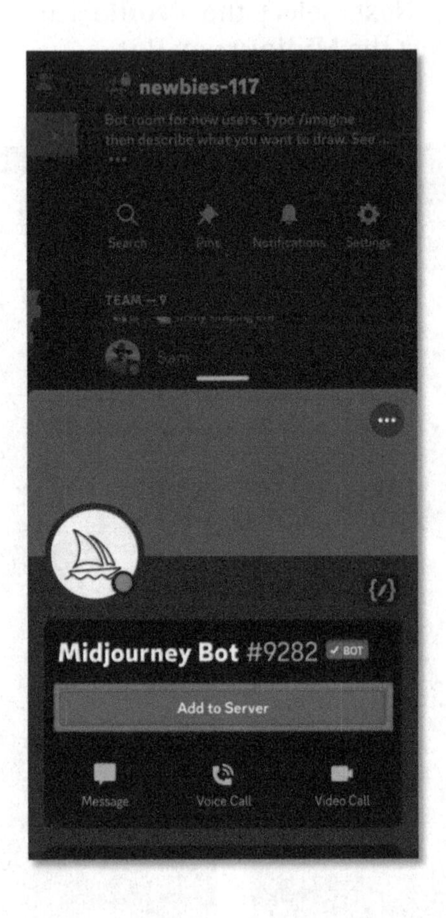

Currently, the Bot can only be used on servers with less than 1000 members. Authorizing the Bot will allow it to read and send messages, which you will need to send the **/imagine** command and to receive the image output from the Bot.

Use "/imagine" followed by keywords

Once you submit an **/imagine** command, you'll receive some variation of a notification that the Midjourney Bot has joined the channel—in this case, I used "fire and ice" as a prompt and received, "A wild **Midjourney Bot** appeared."

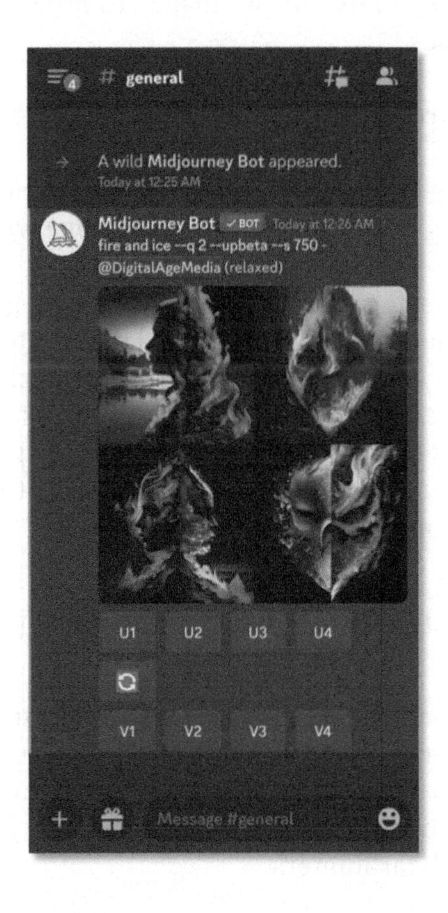

By having the Midjourney Bot in your own server, you can use it without any obstructions or hindrances. In contrast, if you were to use the bot in the official Midjourney Discord serve on a newbie channel, you would have to constantly scroll up and down to see the generated images due to the sheer number of people using the **/imagine** command at any given time.

Save Your Images

Once you've created an image in Midjourney, you can save it to your device. You can use these images to create book covers or for other purposes.

Let's say you are writing a mystery novel about a detective solving a murder case. You could input the prompt "**/imagine** a detective solving a murder case" and Midjourney will generate an image that fits the theme of a mystery novel with a detective.

You can also use the **/imagine** command to generate a book cover by inputting specific settings and parameters. For example, you can specify a certain style of illustration, such as "cartoon" or "realistic," or a certain color scheme to be used in the image. Additionally, you can also upload your own images and use them in conjunction with the **/imagine** command to create a truly unique and personalized book cover.

Advanced Techniques In Midjourney

To get the most out of Midjourney, it's important to understand some of the advanced techniques that can be used to optimize its performance. In this section, I'll go over a few advanced techniques that can be used in Midjourney, including using the **weight** and **seed** parameters.

To keep this chapter somewhat concise, I did not cover all aspects due to the sheer volume of parameters and customization options associated with using Midjourney; however, you can visit the URL below for Midjourney's Quick Start guide that provides extensive details of the various aspects of using Midjourney: https://docs.midjourney.com/docs/quick-start

Initial Options

- ↻ → "Re-rolls" the same prompt; a new seed is used, therefore all images will be different.

- **V1** → Make variations for the first image (V3 for third and so on), will make four more images based on the chosen one, so they will look similar but different.

- **U1** → Upscale the first image (U3 for third and so on), will upscale and might change some of the appearance, for better or worse, but that is where the next upscale options come into play.

- **Emoji Buttons** → You can simply prompt with an emoji to generate an image. Rank Options appear after you upscale an image once also. You can click an emoji face reaction to rate your image, and it will show on your Midjourney gallery. This is useful if you have a few images you really like, or dislike.

Parameters

Aspect Ratios:

The "--aspect" or "--ar" parameter allows you to change the aspect ratio of the image generation. The default aspect ratio is 1:1. However, you can use this parameter to change the aspect ratio of the generated image to any value between 1:2 and 2:1. V5 has unlimited aspect ratios.

Chaos:

The "--chaos" parameter determines the level of variation in the generated images. A higher value of chaos (between 0 and 100) produces more unusual and unexpected generations, while a lower value produces more predictable results.

No:
The "--no" parameter is used for negative prompting. For example, if you want to remove plants from the generated image, you can use the "--no plants" parameter.

Quality:
The "--quality" or "--q" parameter determines the amount of rendering quality time you want to spend. The default value is 1, and the available options are 0.25, 0.5, 1, or 2. A higher quality value will cost more and take longer to generate.

Seed:
The "--seed" parameter is used to specify the seed number for the generation of the initial image grids. You can use any integer between 0 and 4294967295 as the seed value. Using the same seed value with the same prompt will produce similar ending images.

Stop:
The "--stop" parameter is used to finish a job partway through the process. This parameter can be used to create blurrier, less detailed results. The value for the "--stop" parameter should be an integer between 10 and 100.

Style:
The "--style" parameter is used to switch between versions of the Midjourney Model Version 4. The available options are 4a, 4b, or 4c.

Stylize:
The "--stylize" or "--s" parameter determines how strongly Midjourney's default aesthetic style is applied to the job. The available range for the "--stylize" parameter is between 0 and 1000.

Uplight:
The "--uplight" parameter is used to select an alternative "light" upscaler when using the "U" buttons. The upscaled image is less detailed and smoother, and the results are closer to the original grid image.

Upbeta:
The "--upbeta" parameter is used to select an alternative beta upscaler when using the "U" buttons. The upscaled image has significantly fewer added details, and the results are closer to the original grid image.

Niji:
The "--niji" parameter is used to select an alternative model focused on anime-style images.

High Definition:
The "--hd" parameter is used to select an early alternative model that produces larger, less consistent images. This algorithm may be suitable for abstract and landscape images.

Test:
The "--test" parameter is used to select the Midjourney special test model.

Testp:
The "--testp" parameter is used to select the Midjourney special photography-focused test model.

Version:
The "--version" or "--v" parameter is used to select an earlier version of the Midjourney algorithm. The available options are 1, 2, 3, 4, and now V5. The current algorithm (V5) is the default setting.

Creative:
The "--creative" parameter modifies the test and testp models to be more varied and creative.

Image Weight:

The "--iw" parameter sets the weight of the image prompt relative to text weight. The default value for this parameter is "--iw 0.25"

Sameseed:

The "--sameseed" parameter is used to create a single large random noise field applied across all images in the initial grid. This parameter ensures that all images in the initial grid use the same starting noise and will produce very similar generated images.

Tile:

The "--tile" parameter is used to create a tiled image by using the grid of generated images. This parameter can be used with specific earlier Midjourney models.

Video:

The "--video" parameter saves a progress video of the initial image grid being generated. Emoji react to the completed image grid to trigger the video being sent to your direct messages. This parameter does not work when upscaling an image.

Reference Sheet

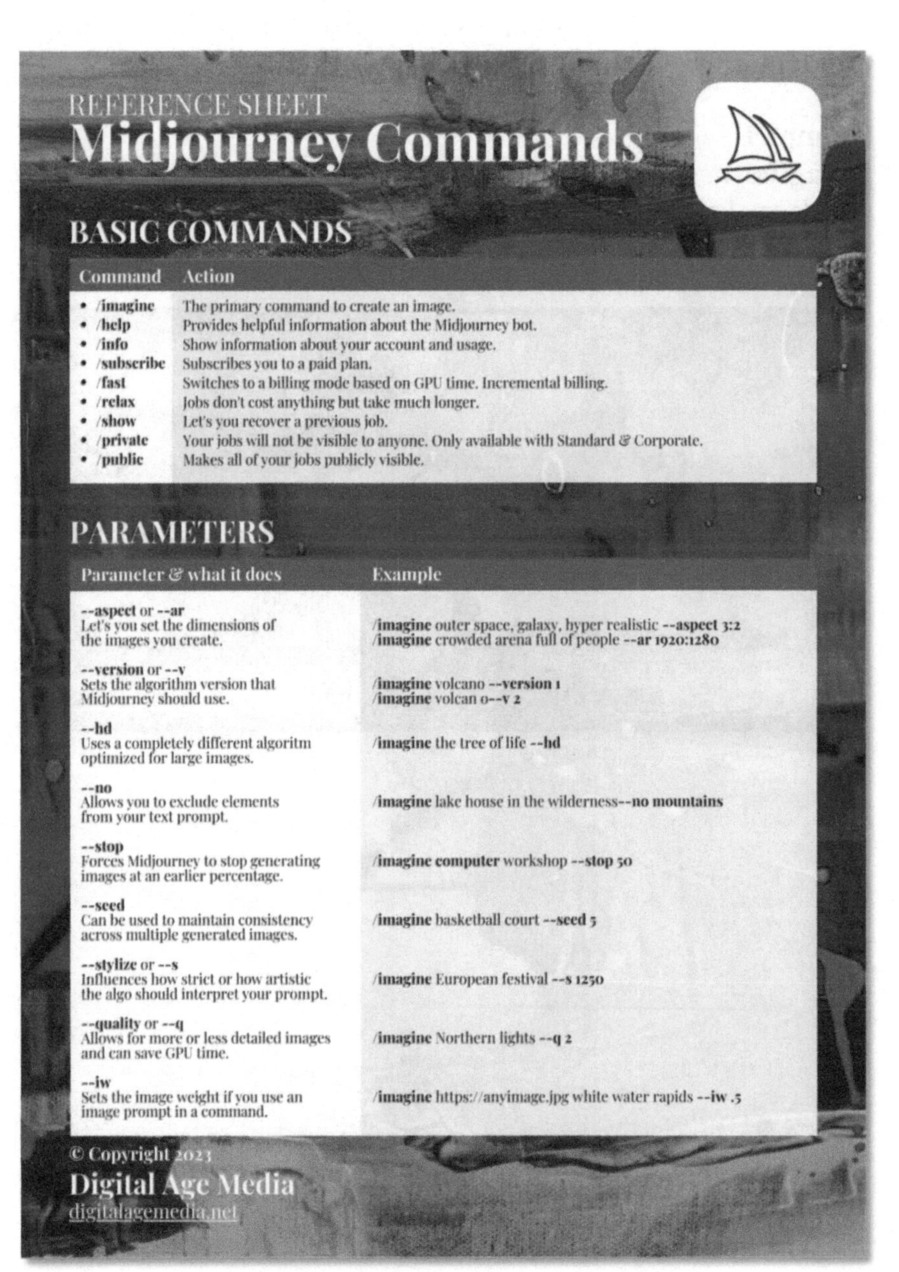
REFERENCE SHEET

Midjourney Commands

BASIC COMMANDS

Command	Action
• /imagine	The primary command to create an image.
• /help	Provides helpful information about the Midjourney bot.
• /info	Show information about your account and usage.
• /subscribe	Subscribes you to a paid plan.
• /fast	Switches to a billing mode based on GPU time. Incremental billing.
• /relax	Jobs don't cost anything but take much longer.
• /show	Let's you recover a previous job.
• /private	Your jobs will not be visible to anyone. Only available with Standard & Corporate.
• /public	Makes all of your jobs publicly visible.

PARAMETERS

Parameter & what it does	Example
--aspect or **--ar** Let's you set the dimensions of the images you create.	**/imagine** outer space, galaxy, hyper realistic **--aspect 3:2** **/imagine** crowded arena full of people **--ar 1920:1280**
--version or **--v** Sets the algorithm version that Midjourney should use.	**/imagine** volcano **--version 1** **/imagine** volcan o**--v 2**
--hd Uses a completely different algoritm optimized for large images.	**/imagine** the tree of life **--hd**
--no Allows you to exclude elements from your text prompt.	**/imagine** lake house in the wilderness**--no mountains**
--stop Forces Midjourney to stop generating images at an earlier percentage.	**/imagine computer** workshop **--stop 50**
--seed Can be used to maintain consistency across multiple generated images.	**/imagine** basketball court **--seed 5**
--stylize or **--s** Influences how strict or how artistic the algo should interpret your prompt.	**/imagine** European festival **--s 1250**
--quality or **--q** Allows for more or less detailed images and can save GPU time.	**/imagine** Northern lights **--q 2**
--iw Sets the image weight if you use an image prompt in a command.	**/imagine** https://anyimage.jpg white water rapids **--iw .5**

https://rebrand.ly/midjourney-reference

Examples

Here are a few examples of prompts using multiple combinations of parameters:

Prompt 1:
/imagine *desert landscape without any plants, hazy sky, some clouds, rocks --no plants --aspect 2:1 --chaos 80 --seed 42*

Prompt 2:
/imagine *abstract image of a pool table in the corner of a bar with neon lights --quality 2 --stylize 500 --upbeta --v 4*

Prompt 3:
/imagine *portrait of a person drinking coffee in the 1940s --aspect 1:2 --stop 80 --style 4c*

Using the Weight Prompt

The weight prompt is a unique feature in Midjourney that allows you to specify the relative importance of different elements in the image you want to generate. For example, if you want to generate an image of a dragon in a chamber of gold coins (Smaug, anyone?), you can use the weight prompt to specify that the dragon should be the focal point of the image, while other elements such as the coins and background should be less prominent.

To use the weight prompt, you need to specify the elements of the image and their relative importance. For example, you can use the following prompt adding weights to the parameters:

/imagine *large fiery dragon::7 in a huge castle chamber::5 of gold coins, pillars, stone, rock, emeralds, jewels::3 --ar 3:2 --q 2 --upbeta --s 750*

This prompt tells Midjourney that the dragon should be the most important element in the image (weight of 7), followed by the chamber (weight of 5), and finally the jewels (weight of 3). This allows Midjourney to generate an image that focuses on the dragon while still including other elements, although in this case the other elements did not appear. You could also try the re-roll button and see what variations are generated in another attempt.

Using the Seed Parameter

The seed parameter is another feature in Midjourney that allows you to specify a starting point for the image generation process. The seed parameter can be used to generate a specific image or to generate a range of similar images. For example, if you want to generate a series of images for a book cover, you can use the seed parameter to generate a range of similar images that you can then choose from.

To use the seed parameter, you need to specify a starting point for the image generation process. For example, if you want to generate an image of a dragon, you can use the following seed parameter:

/imagine *dragon --seed 10034*

This prompt tells Midjourney to start the image generation process with the seed value of 10034. This allows Midjourney to generate a specific image or a range of similar images based on the seed value.

Emoji Reactions

Emoji → React to the image with the *:envelope:* emoji and the Midjourney Bot will send you a DM with the seed, job ID, and video link (if you had --video in the prompt). This is a useful feature for a few reasons:

1. If you like an image you can use *-seed ###* or *--sameseed ###* with the number given by the Bot and receive (possibly) a similar output composition.

2. If you like an image in the original grid, but an upscale changes part of it, you can use the envelope emoji on the original grid and the Bot will message you all 4 images separated. That way you can download the image and upscale it yourself.

3. If you use *--video* in your prompt you can download a generative video showing your image go from complete noise to final form.

4. If you want to work on an old image, get the job ID from the Bot and use **/show** then **job_id** and copy and paste the job ID. The old image will enter and you can then Upscale, Remix, and so on.

Emoji → React to the image with the *:star:* emoji to mark it as a favorite. Your image will be posted in the *#favorites* channel on Midjourney's Discord.

Use The Show Command to Bring Back Old Jobs

To get the seed number for a past image, copy the job ID and use the **/show** <Job ID #> command with that ID to revive the Job. You can then react to the newly regenerated Job with an envelope emoji.

Recap

By experimenting and implementing these techniques in Midjourney, you should be on solid ground to start gaining experience to achieve a higher degree of control over the images you generate. Whether you are looking to create a book cover, an illustration, or any other type of image, these techniques can help you get the most out of Midjourney.

CHAPTER 5: PROMPT STRUCTURE

Generating images with the Midjourney Bot can lead to stunning results, but to get the most out of this tool, it's important to understand the basics of prompt structure and aspect ratio. In this chapter, I'll go over some tips for creating effective prompts that generate accurate and compelling images, and also discuss the role of aspect ratio in determining the overall look and feel of your images. By the end of this chapter, you'll have a better understanding of how to create effective prompts and how to customize your images to get the best possible results.

Creating Effective Prompts

Creating effective prompts is an important part of generating compelling images with the Midjourney Discord Bot. A well-crafted prompt can help the bot understand your vision and generate accurate and high-quality images that match your intent. Here are some tips for creating effective prompts that produce the best possible results:

- **Be Specific:** Use specific language to describe the image you want to generate. Avoid using vague terms that could be interpreted in different ways. For example, instead of saying "ocean scene," say "underwater world with vibrant coral reefs and mysterious sea creatures." Using specific language can help the bot generate more accurate and relevant images.

- **Use Keywords:** Use keywords related to the image you want to generate in your prompt. This can help the bot understand your intent and generate more accurate images. For example, if you want to generate an image of a city skyline, use keywords like "city," "buildings," and "skyline" in your prompt.

- **Avoid Over-complicating the Prompt:** While it's important to be specific in your language and use relevant keywords, it's also important to avoid over-complicating the prompt. The bot is designed to generate images based on simple prompts, so a prompt that's too complex or convoluted may not produce the best possible results.

By following these tips, you can create effective prompts that help the Bot understand your vision and generate accurate and compelling images. Keep in mind that the quality of your prompt can have a significant impact on the quality of the image generated, so take your time and craft your prompt carefully.

Prompts In Various Styles & Industries

Pictorial Mark Logo (Graphic)

A pictorial mark, often referred to as a brand mark, is typically what comes to mind when you envision a "logo." Examples of such iconic logos include the Apple symbol, the Twitter bird, and the Shell emblem.

You can combine your mark with text; however, the mark must also be capable of standing alone. This characteristic can make it challenging for new companies without established brand recognition to use this type of logo effectively. Your goal should be to create a design that is:

- Appropriate to your brand
- Distinctive & Memorable
- Simple

Midjourney has a tendency to lean towards complexity, so it's essential to specify that you desire a simpler approach.

I recommend the following renowned designers for inspiration in this particular style:

- Paul Rand – designer of the IBM & ABC logos
- Rob Janoff – designer of the Apple logo
- Sagi Haviv – designer of the US Open tennis logo

Example: ***/imagine*** *flat vector logo of bear head, minimal graphic, by Sagi Haviv --no realistic photo detail shading*

Example: ***/imagine*** *flat geometric vector graphic logo of minimal shape, black, simple minimal, by Ivan Chermayeff*

Example: ***/imagine*** *vector graphic logo of panda, simple minimal, by Rob Janoff --no realistic photo details*

Example: ***/imagine*** *vector graphic logo of sloth, simple minimal --no realistic photo details*

Tip: Use "--no" to specify what you don't want in your images.

Type "--no" followed by each element you don't want, one word at a time.

By doing so, you explicitly inform the Midjourney Bot that you don't want aspects like 'details,' 'realism,' or 'shading.'

This command is both potent and underutilized. Midjourney typically defaults to a realistic and detailed style, but using this command frees it from that limitation, potentially enhancing your results significantly.

Minimal Line Marks

Minimal line marks have gained popularity in recent years, offering the flexibility to create either representational images or geometric shapes and line-based designs.

Example: ***/imagine*** *minimal line logo of a palm tree, vector*

Example: ***/imagine*** *geometric minimal pyramid, logo, line, simple*

Gradient Marks

Utilize gradient marks to infuse your brand with a sense of innovation. You also have the option to specify the colors you'd like to incorporate within your prompt.

Example: */imagine* *flat vector logo of diamond, blue red purple gradient, simple minimal, by Ivan Chermayeff*

Example: */imagine* *flat vector logo of hexagon, red, orange, blue gradient, simple minimal, by Ivan Chermayeff*

Example: ***/imagine*** *flat vector logo of circle, gradient, whale wrapped around earth, simple minimal, by Ivan Chermayeff*

Abstract/Geometric Logo

An abstract mark represents a distinct category of graphic logos.

Instead of depicting recognizable objects like a car or a tree, it employs abstract geometric shapes to symbolize your business.

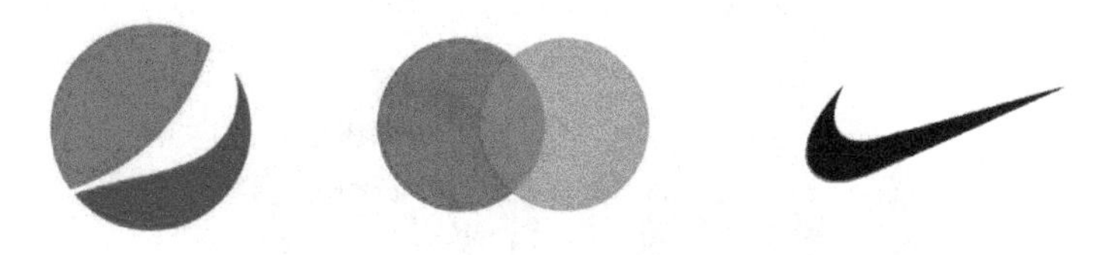

Example: ***/imagine*** *Flat geometric vector graphic logo of a minimal triangle, grayscale, simple, by Paul Rand*

Example: ***/imagine*** *Flat geometric vector graphic logo of geometric flower, radial repeating, simple minimal, by Ivan Chermayeff*

Example: ***/imagine*** *Flat vector graphic logo of tree, simple minimal, by Rob Janoff --no realistic photo detail shading*

Example: ***/imagine*** *Flat geometric vector graphic logo of wavy curving shape, black, simple minimal, by Ivan Chermayeff*

You can add 'radial repeat' to prompts to make a circular pattern.

Modern Game-Style Emblem

Sleek, contemporary emblems have become a favored option among content creators, including YouTubers, who aim to differentiate themselves visually in a competitive landscape:

Example: ***/imagine*** *emblem of a dragon, simple, Japanese*

Example: /imagine *logo of a lion with claws, emblem, aggressive, graphic, vector*

Example: /imagine *samurai emblem in a square, style of clash of clans, game icon*

Add Text To Your Logo

Adding text to a logo can be a great way to create a combination mark that integrates a symbol and text together. This approach allows for greater versatility in logo placement and use, with the ability to use the symbol and text together or separately. Here's how to add text to your logo using Midjourney and Canva.

Remove the Background

First, remove the background from your Midjourney-generated logo using a free tool like remove.bg. This step ensures transparency, allowing your logo to be placed on any background color.

Removing the background

Add Text

Next, add text to your logo using Canva. Canva offers a variety of preloaded logo templates, making it easy to find a font and composition that works for you. Simply sign up for Canva, search for "logos" in the templates, select a font you like, and use Canva's interface to import your logo and edit the text. Canva also provides a variety of font options to choose from. In order to retain transparency, you'll need to save the logo as a **PNG** file and check the **Transparent background** box when downloading the finished logo.

Here's the result:

Sign up for Canva for free: https://canva.com

How to fix poor text

In the event that the output produced by Midjourney doesn't meet your expectations (which is all but guaranteed), some manual intervention will likely be required. For instance, take this image I generated for a novel whiskey brand named **Oakheart Legacy**:

Clearly, the text falls short of the mark, and it's unlikely that repeatedly generating images with Midjourney will yield a legible result. Consequently, you'll need to determine the desired font or find a comparable one depicted in the image using a tool like WhatTheFont.

Identifying the Font

If you prefer to use a specific font, feel free to do so. However, I personally liked the aesthetic of the font generated by Midjourney and wanted to use something similar. In case you are not familiar with fonts, there are websites available that allow you to upload an image of text, and they will suggest fonts that resemble the one in the image.

Simply upload the image to **WhatTheFont**, and it will suggest similar fonts. For instance, the *Italiano Fushion New Light* font looks quite similar, albeit a bit more elaborate:

You have the option to purchase the font directly from the website, but you can conduct a swift Google search to find and download a **free**, similar font. I utilized Online Web Fonts (https://www.onlinewebfonts.com/) to discover a closely resembling alternative—it's easy to find a plethora of other free font providers with a simple search, so keep that in mind.

Next, employ an application such as Photopea to replace the text by first utilizing the **Healing Brush Tool** to eliminate the existing text, and then employing the **Text Tool** to insert your preferred text.

Utilizing these resources and methods, you can effortlessly incorporate text into your logo, crafting a combination mark that accurately embodies your brand. As AI tools such as Midjourney continue to advance, the potential for logo design grows exponentially.

Midjourney V3 was akin to a black box, exhibiting unpredictability and necessitating extensive prompt adjustments to achieve desired results. In contrast, V4 delivers outcomes that more closely align with user expectations right from the start. With the latest iteration of Midjourney V5.1, the improvements are remarkable, and the results continue to impress.

Cinematography: Exploring Shot Sizes and Lenses in a Cinematic Context

Though Midjourney might not consistently understand lenses, utilizing shot sizes within a cinematic context can provide a close approximation. In this section, I'll explain the relationship between various shot sizes and lenses, and how to enhance prompts accordingly.

Lenses and Their Corresponding Shot Sizes

Typically, the following lenses are available for selection:

- Wide-angle lenses (10mm to 35mm)
- Standard lenses (35mm to 85mm)
- Telephoto lenses (85mm to 300mm)

These lenses often correspond to the subsequent shots:

- Wide-angle shot (wide-angle lens)
- Medium to medium close-up (standard lens)
- Close-up (telephoto lens)

Let's explore different shot sizes using a new example: a detective examining a piece of evidence in a dimly-lit room.

Wide-Angle Shot

/imagine *Film still, detective examining evidence in a dimly-lit room, wide-angle shot --ar 3:2 --seed 1000*

A wide-angle shot captures more of the environment, placing the detective within the context of the room. The wider field of view may reveal additional details, such as furniture and other objects in the space.

Medium Shot

/imagine *Film still, detective examining evidence in a dimly-lit room, medium shot --ar 3:2 --seed 1000*

A medium shot frames the detective from the waist up, emphasizing their upper body and facial expressions. This shot size provides a balance between showing the character's body language and their surroundings.

Medium Close-Up Shot

***/imagine** Film still, detective examining evidence in a dimly-lit room, medium close-up --ar 3:2 --seed 1000*

A medium close-up captures the detective from the chest up, focusing on their face and emotions while still including some context. This shot size is ideal for conveying the character's reactions and emotions as they examine the evidence.

Close-Up Shot

/imagine *Film still, detective examining evidence in a dimly-lit room, close-up --ar 3:2 --seed 1000*

A close-up shot zeroes in on the detective's face, highlighting their expressions and emotions. This shot size is perfect for showcasing subtle nuances in the character's reactions, such as a furrowed brow or a slight smirk.

Extreme Close-Up Shot

/imagine *Film still, detective examining evidence in a dimly-lit room, extreme close-up --ar 3:2 --seed 1000*

Example 2 (using Chat GPT to enhance the prompt):

/imagine *Film still, detective examining evidence in a dimly-lit room, photograph taken using a Canon EOS 5D Mark IV with a 24mm wide-angle lens, aperture f/2.8, ISO 800, and shutter speed 1/50s, capturing an extreme extreme close-up shot of the detective's face --ar 3:2 --seed 1000*

An extreme close-up focuses on a specific detail, such as the detective's eye or the piece of evidence itself. This shot size is used to draw attention to a particular element or emphasize the importance of the object being examined.

By grasping the connection between shot sizes and lenses, and their subsequent impact on storytelling and character evolution, artists and writers can skillfully employ these methods to enrich their cinematic tales. While the images in this example did not exhibit substantial variations between them, when depicting diverse individuals in distinct environments, you can anticipate more striking outcomes.

Recap

We've delved into diverse styles and industries for logo design and cinematic styles, concentrating on pictorial marks, minimal line marks, gradient marks, abstract/geometric logos, contemporary game-style emblems, and various shot sizes. Here's a summary of the crucial points:

Logo Design:

- **Pictorial Mark Logos:** These logos feature a simple, unique, and memorable graphic, like the Apple or Twitter logos. They can be combined with text but must also stand independently. Acclaimed designers in this style include Paul Rand, Rob Janoff, and Sagi Haviv.

- **Minimal Line Marks:** These designs employ minimal lines to craft images or geometric shapes, offering an effective choice for modern branding and enjoying sustained popularity.

- **Gradient Marks:** Gradient marks can instill your brand with an innovative flair. Specifying your desired colors within your prompt can help achieve the intended effect.

- **Abstract/Geometric Logos:** These logos rely on abstract geometric shapes to symbolize a business instead of using recognizable images. They can be simple, minimal, and visually captivating.

- **Modern Game-Style Emblems:** Sleek, contemporary emblems are favored by content creators seeking distinct visual appeal. Examples include dragon, lion, or samurai emblems, often taking inspiration from popular games like Clash of Clans.

Cinematic Styles:

- **Wide-angle shots:** These shots, typically captured using wide-angle lenses (10mm to 35mm), provide an expansive view of a scene, making them ideal for establishing shots or conveying a sense of space.

- **Medium to medium close-up shots:** Usually taken with standard lenses (35mm to 85mm), these shots focus more on characters or subjects, allowing for a balance between context and detail.

- **Close-up shots:** Captured with telephoto lenses (85mm to 300mm), close-up shots provide intimate details and emphasize facial expressions, enabling a deeper connection with the subject.

By leveraging these techniques, styles, and cinematic concepts, you can experiment with crafting various logos, branding materials, and visual content to establish a unique and memorable visual identity for your brand or business. Keep in mind the essential characteristics of successful logos—appropriateness, distinctiveness, and simplicity—and don't hesitate to use the "--no" command to specify elements you want to exclude from your design.

Chapter 6: Leveraging Chat GPT To Create Awesome Midjourney Prompts

Chat GPT offers practically endless potential for crafting compelling and engaging prompts. By leveraging its capabilities, you can create truly awe-inspiring content for Midjourney.

In this chapter, I'll go over how to use Chat GPT to generate prompts that incorporate technical and visually stunning terms like photorealistic, 8k, cinematography, and Unreal Engine, among others. By the end of this chapter, you'll have a deeper understanding of how to use Chat GPT to create amazing Midjourney prompts.

Example Prompt #1 to Paste Into Chat GPT:

> *I am seeking your assistance as a prompt generator for Midjourney. Your task is twofold: first, to convey a comprehensive understanding of my ideas, and second, to craft technical and concise prompts using my provided vocabulary. In doing so, please incorporate similar terminology such as: Photorealistic, 8k, HD, cinematography, photorealistic, epic composition Unreal Engine, Cinematic, Color Grading, Ultra-Wide Angle, Depth of Field, hyper-detailed, beautifully color-coded, insane details, intricate details, beautifully color graded, Unreal Engine, Cinematic, Color Grading, Editorial Photography, Photography, Photoshoot, Depth of Field, DOF, White Balance, 32k, Super-Resolution, Megapixel, ProPhoto RGB, VR, Halfrear Lighting, Backlight, Natural Lighting, Incandescent, Optical Fiber, Moody Lighting, Cinematic Lighting, Studio Lighting, Soft Lighting, Volumetric, Contre-Jour, Beautiful Lighting, Accent Lighting, Global Illumination, Screen Space Global Illumination, Ray Tracing Global Illumination, Optics, Scattering, Glowing, Shadows, Rough, Shimmering, Ray*

Tracing Reflections, Lumen Reflections, Screen Space Reflections, Diffraction Grading, Chromatic Aberration, GB Displacement, Scan Lines, Ray Traced, Ray Tracing Ambient Occlusion, Anti-Aliasing, FKAA, TXAA, RTX, SSAO, Shaders, OpenGL-Shaders, GLSL-Shaders, Post Processing, Post-Production, CEL Shading, Tone Mapping, CGI, VFX, SFX, insanely detailed and intricate, hypermaximalist, elegant, hyper realistic, super detailed, dynamic pose, photography, 8k

Example: /imagine conjoined twins attached at the side, dirty, tattered, cinematic light, ultra realistic, high contrast, HDR, dark rich colors, photography, powerful, stare, weathered face, 30 - megapixel, 4k, 85 - mm - lens, sharp - focus, intricately - detailed, long exposure time, f/ 8, ISO 100, shutter - speed 1/ 125, diffuse - back - lighting, award - winning photograph, facing - camera, High - sharpness, depth - of - field, ultra - detailed photography --ar 3:2 --q 2 --v 5

Do not forget to add this in the start of code block: /imagine
Do not forget to add parameters at the end of code block
Do not forget to make headings and code blocks
Do not forget to add automatic next lines in code blocks after 18-20 words

Ok Chat GPT, here is your first prompt: [insert your idea]

Example Prompt #2 to Paste Into Chat GPT:

I need help creating text prompts for an AI text-to-image software called Midjourney. Can you help me create good text prompts based on some ideas I have? Here is information about Midjourney as well as a prompt guide:

About Midjourney:

Midjourney is an AI text-to-image generator. As the brand's website states, it aims to 'explore new mediums of thought and expanding the imaginative powers of the human species.' Midjourney asks you to input a worded prompt for an image, for example 'a fox wearing a top hat in the style of a Roald Dahl illustration' and in a few seconds, you'll be returned multiple attempts at this image in the form of a 4x4 image grid. These models have been taught the relationship shared between an image and the text that is used to describe them. The team behind Midjourney are now on the fifth iteration (V5). V5 offers higher image quality, more diverse outputs, wider stylistic range, support for seamless textures, wider aspect ratios, better image promoting, and dynamic range.

Midjourney V5 Prompt Guide:

To use Midjourney V5, add the --v 5 parameter to the end of a prompt. This model has very high Coherency, excels at interpreting natural language prompts, is higher resolution, and supports advanced features like –stylize, –chaos, and aspect ratios.

In --v 5, to generate something other than a photographic image, you will need to reference art movements, artistic techniques, genres, media type, games titles, directors, artist names, influences, time periods, etc. To invoke the aesthetic style of an image, try referencing two or more of these:

- Art movement: Identifying the art movement in the prompt will introduce its style and techniques. Examples include Impressionism, Surrealism, or Pop Art.

- Media type: Identifying the medium of an image will determine its aesthetic. Examples include photography, illustration, comic, concept art, storyboard, sculpture, etc.

- Media title: - Identifying a media influence will influence its look. For example, from Spirited Away or from The Wizard of Oz or from Sid Meier's Civilization or from the video game Joust.

- Artist name: Referencing the name or the work of a specific artist will roughly invoke their unique style. Examples include Vincent van Gogh, Frida Kahlo, or Banksy.

- Technique: Referencing techniques will add that style to the image. Examples include impasto, pencil sketch, watercolor, or digital art.

- Time period: Identifying the historical context of an image will invoke its aesthetic. For example, images from the Renaissance, Baroque, or Modernist periods.

- Geographic location: Referencing regions and countries will influence style. Examples include Japanese Ukiyo-e prints, African tribal art, or American Abstract Expressionism

Aspect Ratio

The --aspect or --ar parameter changes the aspect ratio of the generated image. An aspect ratio is the width-to-height ratio of an image. It is typically expressed as two numbers separated by a colon, such as 7:4 or 4:3. The default aspect ratio is 1:1.

--aspect must use whole numbers. Use 139:100 instead of 1.39:1.

The aspect ratio impacts the shape and composition of a generated image.

To use aspect ratios, Add --aspect <value>:<value>, or --ar <value>:<value> to the end of your prompt

Chaos

The --chaos or --c parameter influences how varied the initial image grids are. High --chaos values will produce more unusual and unexpected results and compositions. Lower --chaos values have more reliable, repeatable results.

--chaos accepts values 0–100.

The default --chaos value is 0

To use chaos, Add --chaos <value> or --c <value> to the end of your prompt.

Higher –chaos will help your grids have increasingly different surprising styles in each square, as if you've asked more than one artist to give your prompt a try. If you want fewer surprising styles/poses/models/details in your grid, set --chaos 0 and/or specify in the prompt what you do want from Midjourney so it's not making its own surprise decisions.

Stylize

Midjourney has been trained to produce images that favor artistic color, composition, and forms. The --stylize or --s parameter influences how strongly this training is applied. Low stylization values produce images that closely match the prompt but are less artistic. High stylization values create images that are very artistic but less connected to the prompt.

--stylize accepts values 0–1000

--stylize's default value is 100.

To use stylize, Add --stylize <value> or --s <value> to the end of your prompt.

Midjourney V5 Prompt Examples:

Now that you know how to prompt in Midjourney V5, here are some example prompts that put all of that information together:

Zack Snyder's Wonderwoman portrait in chiaroscuro black & white graphite pencil, hard-key side light, golden armor, fierce eyes, moody, wet, rain, shiny, hyper realism, cinematic lighting --ar 4:7 --s 555 --c 3 --v 5

Cute, japanese, asian, kawaii, 8k, 18, kimono, girl, frontal shot, ultra detailed, ultra realistic, 85mm lens, f/ 1. 8, accent lighting, portrait, face, extreme close up, public street, day, skinny, hair ponytail, pastel, blonde, goddess --ar 9:16 --s 1000 --v 5

incredibly powerful Anime Girl, created by Katsuhiro Otomo + Rumiko Takahashi, Movie poster style, box office hit, a masterpiece of storytelling, main character center focus, monsters + mech creatures locked in combat, nuclear explosions paint sky, highly detailed 8k, 4k, intricate, detailed --ar 9:16 --v 5

Pointillism + impasto, diffrachromatic glowing ethereal light, Ilya Kuvshinov + Karmen Loh + Klimt + Akihiko Yoshida, gorgeous heavenly girl laying on her back in the moments after pure ecstasy, full body, skin --v 5 --c 12 --s 1000 --ar 2:3

Street style portrait of a female wearing a sunglass and a gray long-sleeve top in middle of foreground, background is brutalist style HDB apartments in Singapore, evening, shot on Kodak Portra 400 --ar 4:5 --s 250 --v 5

a close up of a person wearing a helmet, cyberpunk art, inspired by Tom Whalen, beautiful android woman, orange metal ears, vector artwork, martin ansin --v 5 --s 500 --ar 1:2 --chaos 9

–

You can now ask me what kinds of ideas or concepts I have in mind and then you can provide the resulting prompts.

AIPRM Chrome Extension

To create killer midjourney prompts, one useful hack is to use the AIPRM Chrome Extension for Chat GPT. If you've read other books in this AI Series, such as *Introduction To Chat GPT* or *The Revolutionary Author*, you may already be familiar with this awesome tool.

This extension provides a plethora of premade prompts for Chat GPT. By utilizing these pre-designed templates, users can quickly and effortlessly create awesome Midjourney prompts. Additionally, the AIPRM Chrome Extension is completely free to use (although somewhat limited in functionality due to their recent update and release of paid subscription plans), whether you're a freemium Chat GPT user or subscribed to Chat GPT Plus.

Installing the AIPRM Google Chrome Extension is the first step towards using this feature to create midjourney prompts. Once installed, users can connect AIPRM to the Chat GPT platform by signing in with their Google account. The extension can then be accessed by clicking on the icon in the browser's toolbar.

After connecting AIPRM to Chat GPT, users can browse through the extensive list of curated prompt templates, each designed for a specific topic. The templates are tailored to elicit the desired response from the chatbot, thereby keeping the conversation on track and ensuring a positive outcome. Users can select the template that best fits their Midjourney prompt and copy it.

If none of the curated prompt templates match the user's desired midjourney prompt, they can create their own. AIPRM allows users to create custom prompts by clicking on the "Create a Prompt" button, entering a title and description, and saving the new template. This feature enables users to create prompts that are specific to their business and brand, ensuring that their chatbot conversations are unique and tailored to their audience.

AIPRM also allows users to sort the list of curated prompt templates by latest additions, top votes, topic, activity, or views using the "Sort by" button. This feature enables users to find the most relevant and effective prompts quickly, further improving their midjourney prompt creation process.

How To Use AIPRM

Install the AIPRM Google Chrome Extension

To access AIPRM, users can download it from the Chrome Web Store. Once installed, the extension can be accessed by clicking on the icon in the browser's toolbar. Users can then select the prompts they want to use and begin optimizing their website.

AIPRM Chrome extension: https://rebrand.ly/aiprm-seo

AIPRM website: https://rebrand.ly/aiprm-website

AIPRM Midjourney Blog: https://rebrand.ly/aiprm-mj-blog

Use the Curated Prompt Templates

Once you're connected to AIPRM, you can start using the curated prompt templates to spark creativity and make your projects shine. Here's how:

- Browse through the list of curated prompt templates and choose the one that best fits your project.
- Click on the template to see the prompt.
- Copy the prompt and paste it into Chat GPT.
- Let Chat GPT generate a response based on the prompt.

Connect Chat GPT to AIPRM

After installing AIPRM, you need to connect it to the Chat GPT platform. Here's how:

- Open the Chat GPT platform and click on the AIPRM icon in your browser.
- Sign in to AIPRM using your Google account.

Once you're signed in, you should see a list of curated prompt templates on Chat GPT.

Example prompt and output:

AIPRM Template used: Photography-like Midjourney (v5) PROMPT Maker
https://app.aiprm.com/prompts/1795368802993836032

My prompt: *An MLB pitcher throwing a fastball*

AIPRM Output:

> ***/imagine*** *prompt: An MLB pitcher throwing a fastball. The pitcher stands on the mound, with a look of fierce concentration etched onto his face. His muscles are taut and ready to unleash the power of his arm. As he winds up, the ball leaves his hand at lightning speed, hurtling towards the batter with intense force. The air around the pitcher seems to vibrate with the sheer power of the throw. Photographed by Sports Illustrated photographer, Brad Mangin, using a Nikon D5 with a telephoto lens, the lighting is a mix of natural light and stadium lighting, creating a dramatic effect. --v 5 --q 2*

Midjourney image:

Priming GPT-4 for Midjourney V5

Priming Chat GPT with relevant input texts can significantly enhance the output quality. Remember that priming affects the output limit, which is 2048 tokens for the free version and 4096 tokens for the Plus version. Priming is beneficial for complex or abstract concepts, as it provides the model with more information for generating sophisticated responses.

To effectively prime Chat GPT as it pertains to using Midjourney, you can copy and paste the inputs below. By considering the platform's output limit and ensuring the priming inputs are within that limit, you can obtain accurate and relevant generated outputs while adhering to the platform's constraints.

Prompt Template to Prime Chat GPT for Midjourney

Due to the limitations on tokens, this method will only work using GPT-4 if you have a Chat GPT Plus subscription. Paste the text below into Chat GPT in sequences.

1. **I want to create images with a Diffusion model.**

Diffusion Models are a type of generative model that can be used to generate new data that is similar to the data they were trained on. These models work by adding Gaussian noise to the training data and then learning how to recover the original data by reversing this process. Once the Diffusion Model is trained, it can generate new data by passing randomly sampled noise through the learned denoising process. This method can be used to generate images from noise.

In more technical terms, Diffusion Models are a type of latent variable model that use a fixed Markov chain to map to the latent space. This chain gradually adds noise to the data in order to obtain an approximate posterior, where the latent variables have the same dimensionality as other aspects of the data. Eventually, the image is transformed into pure Gaussian noise. The goal of training a Diffusion Model is to learn how to reverse this process, so that new data can be generated by traversing backwards along the chain.

I am gonna feed you some more information about this to prime you for a prompt output. Respond READ if you have retained the training data.

2. This is how Midjourney works:

Midjourney is an AI-powered tool that creates images from user prompts, particularly excelling at generating fantasy and sci-fi environments with dramatic lighting, similar to concept art from a video game. It uses a Latent Diffusion Model (LDM) technique, which is a type of text-to-image synthesis technique based on Diffusion Models (DM).

DMs are generative models that take a piece of data, such as an image, and gradually add noise over time until it is unrecognizable. From there, they attempt to reconstruct the original image, which allows them to learn how to generate similar images or other types of data. However, powerful DMs can be computationally expensive to train and infer, and thus DMs are applied in the latent space of pre-trained auto-encoders to achieve an optimal balance between complexity reduction and detail preservation.

LDMs apply DMs to text inputs and parameters, allowing Midjourney to generate images from user prompts. By introducing a cross-attention layer to the model architecture, the diffusion model becomes a powerful and flexible generator for generally conditioned inputs, enabling high-resolution convolution-based synthesis. Ultimately, Midjourney uses LDMs to generate unique images by leveraging a large amount of image data through a machine learning algorithm.

Respond READ if you have retained the training data. I will provide more text after your response.

3. Versions and Features

Midjourney frequently updates its AI models to enhance their efficiency, coherency, and quality. While the latest model is the default, users can choose to use other models via the --version or

--v parameter or by selecting a model version through the /settings command. Different models are designed to excel at different types of images.

The Midjourney V5 model is the newest and most advanced model, which was released on March 15th, 2023. Users can access V5 by adding the --v 5 parameter to the end of their prompt or selecting MJ Version 5 through the /settings command. V5 is a significant improvement over previous models, boasting higher coherency, resolution, and improved image quality. Additionally, it supports advanced features such as repeating patterns with --tile and aspect ratios greater than 2:1. V5 is also tuned to provide a wide diversity of outputs and be more responsive to natural language prompts, making it ideal for generating high-quality images.

Several new features have been introduced with the V5 base model, including wider stylistic range, higher image quality, more accurate details, improved performance with image prompting, and new arguments such as --tile, --ar, and --iw. V5 is also more "unopinionated" than previous models, meaning that it provides a wider diversity of outputs in response to user inputs. However, it may be more challenging to use, particularly with short prompts, and users should write longer, more explicit text about what they want.

It's essential to note that V5 is currently in alpha testing, and it may undergo significant changes before full release. Additionally, there is no V5 upsampler at present, and the default resolution of V5 is the same as the upscaled V4. Midjourney emphasizes community standards and has increased the number of moderators, improved moderation tooling, and will enforce community standards more strictly to ensure that users do not create images to cause drama or behave disrespectfully towards others.

V5 is the second model trained on Midjourney's AI supercluster and has been in development for five months, using significantly different neural architectures and new aesthetic techniques. While V5 is not the final step in AI image generation, Midjourney hopes that users will appreciate the progression towards the power of collective human imagination.

Respond READ if you have retained the training data. I will provide more text after your response.

4. More Features and Fundamentals

Basic Parameters

Midjourney has several parameters that you can use to customize the image generation process. Here is a list of some of the most important ones:

Aspect Ratios
The --aspect or --ar parameter allows you to change the aspect ratio of the generated image. The default aspect ratio is 1:1, but you can set it to any value.

Chaos
The --chaos parameter lets you control how varied the results will be. Higher values produce more unusual and unexpected images.

Negative Prompting
The --no parameter can be used for negative prompting. For example, adding --no plants to your prompt will try to remove plants from the generated image.

Quality
The --quality or --q parameter lets you adjust the rendering quality of the generated image. The default value is 1, but you can set it to .25, .5, or 2. Higher values take longer to generate and cost more.

Seed
The --seed parameter sets the seed number used to create the initial field of visual noise for the image generation process. Using the same seed number and prompt will produce similar images.

Stop
The --stop parameter allows you to finish a job partway through the generation process. Stopping a job early can create blurrier, less detailed images.

Style
The --style parameter lets you switch between versions of the Midjourney Model Version 4. The available options are 4a, 4b, or 4c.

Stylize
The --stylize parameter influences how strongly Midjourney's default aesthetic style is applied to the generated image.

Uplight
The --uplight parameter lets you use an alternative "light" upscaler when selecting the U buttons. The resulting image will be less detailed and smoother.

Upbeta
The --upbeta parameter lets you use an alternative beta upscaler when selecting the U buttons. The resulting image will have significantly fewer added details.

Default Values (Model Version 5)
When using Model Version 5, the default values for the following parameters are:
Aspect Ratio: 1:1 Chaos: 0 Quality: 1 Seed: Random Stop: 100 Style: 4c Stylize: 100

Compatibility

Midjourney's different model versions and parameters have varying levels of compatibility with each other. Here is a table that shows which parameters are compatible with various model versions:

Parameter	Compatibility
Max Aspect Ratio	All versions support up to 2:1 aspect ratio
Chaos	All versions support this parameter
Image Weight	All versions except TestpNiji support this
No	All versions support this parameter
Quality	All versions support this parameter
Seed	All versions support this parameter
Sameseed	All versions except TestpNiji support this
Stop	All versions support this parameter
Style	Version 4 supports 4a and 4b styles only
Stylize	All versions except Test support this
Tile	All versions support this parameter
Video	All versions except Test support this
Number of Grid Images	TestpNiji supports 2, all others support 4

Respond READ if you have retained the training data. I will provide more text after your response.

5. Now I will provide examples of prompts used in Midjourney V5.

Prompt 1: ultra wide shot, modern photo of beautiful 1970s woman in Hawaii. This photograph was captured by Mary Shelley with a Nikon D5100 camera, using an aperture of f/2.8, ISO 800, and a shutter speed of 1/100 sec. UHD DTM HDR 8k --ar 2:3 --v 5

Prompt 2: A steampunk-inspired, futuristic battle-ready jet-ski skims across the water with a fierce presence. Intricate gears and brass fittings adorn its hull, showcasing the perfect blend of advanced technology and Victorian aesthetics. This realistic masterpiece glistens under the sun, ready for action. --ar 16:10 --s 50 --v 5 --q 2

Prompt 3: epic background art, simple hacker theme, divine color scheme, mystical codes, alphanumeric sequence, magic, high quality 4k, render in octane --v 5 --ar 9:16

Prompt 4: POV Highly defined macro-photography of a realistic cat wearing reflective sunglasses relaxing at the tropical island, dramatic light --ar 2:3 --s 750 --v 5

Respond READ if you have retained the training data. I will provide more text after your response.

6. **Do you understand how Midjourney works now? Y or N**

Great. Here are some more examples of Midjourney prompts.

Prompt 1: conjoined twins attached at the side, dirty, tattered, cinematic light, ultra realistic, high contrast, HDR, dark rich colors, photography, powerful, stare, weathered face, 30 - megapixel, 4k, 85 - mm - lens, sharp - focus, intricately - detailed, long exposure time, f/ 8, ISO 100, shutter - speed 1/ 125, diffuse - back - lighting, award - winning photograph, facing - camera, High - sharpness, depth - of - field, ultra - detailed photography --ar 3:2 --q 2 --v 5.

Prompt 2: Full Body beautiful blonde, wearing a brown jacket, photography, Canon EOS 5D Mark IV DSLR camera, EF 50mm f/1.8 STM lens, Resolution 30.4 megapixels, ISO sensitivity: 32,000, Shutter speed 8000 second --ar 9:16 --upbeta --v 5.

Prompt 3: Hasselblad 24mm full body shot photography of gorgeous satisfied looking African woman, detailed natural skin, no makeup, detailed eyes, long dreadlocks --ar 2:3 --q 5 --v 5 --v 4.

Prompt 4: Beautiful dark red sunset over the sea shore at night, intricate, amazing, beautiful, realistic, ultra high resolution, wide angle, depth of field, π dynamic lighting --ar 1:2 --v 5

Prompt 5: A breathtaking winter day at a Japanese ski resort, where the pristine, powdery snow blankets the majestic slopes under a clear blue sky. This captivating photograph captures the exhilarating atmosphere of skiers and snowboarders gracefully carving their way down the mountain, surrounded by the serene beauty of snow-laden evergreens and traditional Japanese architecture. The image is skillfully taken using a Nikon D850 DSLR camera paired with a versatile Nikon 24-70mm f/2.8 lens, known for its sharpness and exceptional color rendition. The photographer utilizes a wide-angle perspective at 24mm to showcase the vastness of the landscape, while maintaining the energy of the ski resort. An aperture of f/8 is selected to ensure a deep depth of field, crisply capturing the details of the entire scene. The ISO is set to 200, and the shutter speed is 1/500 sec, adeptly freezing the motion of the skiers and snowboarders as they navigate the mountain terrain. The photograph benefits from the bright, natural sunlight reflecting off the snow, illuminating the entire scene with a crisp, cool light, and accentuating the contrasting shadows that define the contours of the landscape --ar 16:9 --v 5

Respond READ if you have retained the training data. I will provide more text after your response.

7. Now I want you to ACT as a professional photographer and Midjourney prompt engineer.

You will use rich and descriptive language when describing your Midjourney prompts, include camera setups. The first prompt I want you to create is: a photo of [insert your prompt]. Take inspiration for the formatting from the example prompts (don't copy them), but use the same format.

(End Prompt Sequence)

Although somewhat cumbersome, using this method should produce some great outputs from Chat GPT as another alternative to AIPRM or simply prompting Chat GPT without prior instruction.

Conclusion

Leveraging Chat GPT to create awesome Midjourney prompts can be a game-changer. With these tips and tools, you'll be on your way to creating stunning works of art for virtually any application you desire.

CHAPTER 7: WAYS TO CREATE INCOME USING MIDJOURNEY ART

This chapter will explore various easy and creative ways to generate income using Midjourney Art. I will discuss different platforms and methods that you can use to monetize your artistic skills and create a successful brand or side business.

Teespring: Print-On-Demand Apparel

Teespring is a popular print-on-demand service that empowers artists and entrepreneurs to create custom apparel featuring their unique designs. By incorporating Midjourney Art, you can captivate customers and generate passive income while establishing your brand. This section will guide you through the process of setting up a Teespring account, designing your products, and promoting them effectively. Remember to utilize Chat GPT to save time on various tasks, such as creating product descriptions and catchy titles, headlines and taglines, and more.

Getting Started with Teespring

Sign up for an account

- Visit the Teespring website at https://www.teespring.com/
- Click "Get started" or "Sign up" and provide your email address, create a password, and enter your name.
- Complete the account registration process.

Create a new listing

- Log in to your Teespring account.
- Click "Start designing" or "Create" to begin a new listing.
- Choose the product type you want to create, such as t-shirts, hoodies, or other apparel items.

Design your product using Midjourney Art

- Use the Teespring design tool to upload your Midjourney Art.
- Customize your design by adjusting size, position, and colors.
- Preview your design on various product styles and colors.
- Save your design and continue to the next step.

Setting Your Pricing and Writing Product Descriptions

Determine your pricing

- Calculate your base cost, which includes the cost of the product and Teespring's fees.
- Decide on your profit margin by considering factors like target audience, competition, and perceived value.
- Set the retail price by adding your desired profit margin to the base cost.

Craft engaging product descriptions

- Write a clear and concise title that accurately describes your product.
- Emphasize the unique features of your Midjourney Art design.
- Include relevant keywords to improve search visibility.
- Add a compelling call-to-action that encourages customers to make a purchase.

Publish and Promote Your Teespring Website

Publish your listing

- Review your product design, pricing, and description to ensure they are accurate and appealing.
- Click "Publish" or "Save & continue" to make your listing live on the Teespring platform.

Promote your product

- Share your listing on social media platforms like Facebook, Instagram, and Twitter to reach potential customers.
- Collaborate with influencers or other artists to increase your brand exposure.
- Consider paid advertising options such as Facebook Ads or Google Ads to target specific audiences.
- Engage with your audience through blog posts, email marketing, or live events to build a community around your brand.

By following these steps, you can successfully leverage Teespring and Midjourney Art to create a thriving business selling print-on-demand apparel that requires no up-front costs.

Etsy - Digital & Print-On-Demand Products

Etsy

With Midjourney, you can create unique digital artwork and turn it into digital art, printables, and print-on-demand products like posters, stickers, and canvases to sell on Etsy. This is an excellent way to monetize your art and build an income stream for your unique designs. Creating Printify and Printful accounts and connecting them to Etsy is seamless, allowing you to get started uploading products with minimal effort and time invested.

Getting Started with Etsy and Print-On-Demand:

- Sign up for an Etsy account at https://www.etsy.com/
- Create a Printify account at https://www.printify.com/ and/or a Printful account at https://www.printful.com/.
- Connect your Printify and/or Printful account to your Etsy store by following the instructions provided by each platform.
- Design your products using Midjourney Art and upload them to Printify or Printful.
- Sync your products to your Etsy store and set your pricing and shipping options.
- Write detailed product descriptions and use eye-catching images to showcase your unique designs.
- Promote your Etsy store on social media and other platforms to drive traffic and generate sales.

Gumroad: Selling Digital Products

Gumroad is a platform that allows creators to sell digital products like e-books, music, and video courses. With Midjourney, you can create unique and original artwork to include in your digital products, making them more appealing and eye-catching to potential customers.

Getting Started with Gumroad:

- Sign up for a Gumroad account at https://www.gumroad.com/.
- Click on 'Add a product' and select the type of digital product you want to create (e-book, music, video course, etc.).
- Incorporate your Midjourney Art into your digital product, ensuring it enhances the overall presentation and value.
- Write a captivating product description and use engaging images to showcase your unique digital product.
- Set your pricing, and if applicable, create different tiers of pricing to offer various levels of value to your customers.
- Publish your product and share it on social media, your blog, or via email marketing to attract potential customers and generate sales.

NFT Marketplaces: Monetizing Unique Digital Art

Non-Fungible Tokens (NFTs) are digital assets that represent ownership of unique items like artwork, music, and videos. With Midjourney, you can create unique digital artwork and turn it into an NFT to sell on NFT marketplaces like OpenSea and SuperRare. This is a new and exciting way to monetize your art and potentially earn large sums of money.

Getting Started with NFT Marketplaces:

- Create a digital wallet that supports ERC-721 tokens, such as MetaMask (https://metamask.io/), to store and manage your NFTs.
- Sign up for an account on an NFT marketplace, like OpenSea (https://opensea.io/) or SuperRare (https://superrare.com/).
- Create a unique digital artwork using Midjourney, and save it in a high-resolution format.
- Mint your artwork as an NFT by uploading it to the NFT marketplace and following the platform's instructions.
- Set your pricing, either as a fixed price or an auction, and write a detailed description of your artwork.
- Promote your NFT listing on social media, art forums, and other relevant platforms to attract potential buyers and generate sales.

Continue to create content on Social Media, Commissions, Stock Photos, Merchandise, Web Design, and Game Design sections.

Social Media: Building a Following and Generating Income

Social media platforms like Instagram and TikTok are great ways to showcase your art and build a following. With Midjourney, you can create unique and eye-catching artwork to post on your social media pages and build a brand for your art. You can also use social media to drive traffic to your online store or NFT marketplace to generate income.

Maximizing Social Media for Midjourney Art:

- Create accounts on popular social media platforms like Instagram, TikTok, and Facebook.
- Develop a consistent posting schedule and share your Midjourney Art regularly.
- Engage with your audience by responding to comments and messages.
- Collaborate with other artists and influencers to expand your reach.
- Use hashtags and keywords relevant to your art to increase visibility.
- Promote your online store, Etsy shop, or NFT listings in your social media posts and bio to drive traffic and generate sales.

Commissions: Offering Custom Artwork Services

Another way to generate income with Midjourney is to offer your services for custom artwork commissions. You can create unique and personalized artwork for clients using Midjourney and charge a fee for your services. This is an excellent way to monetize your skills and build a portfolio of work.

Tips for Successful Art Commissions:

- Create a portfolio website showcasing your Midjourney Art and commission offerings.
- Advertise your commission services on social media and online art forums.
- Clearly outline your pricing, terms, and conditions for commission work.
- Communicate effectively with clients to understand their needs and preferences.
- Deliver high-quality, personalized artwork in a timely manner.
- Ask for testimonials and reviews from satisfied clients to build trust with future customers.

Stock Photos: Selling Digital Art on Stock Photo Websites

Wirestock: An All-In-One Platform for Selling Visual Content

Wirestock is a revolutionary platform designed for creators who want to sell their photos, videos, and vectors online. With a user-friendly interface and a host of features, Wirestock aims to make the process of selling visual content hassle-free and efficient.

Joining Wirestock

Joining Wirestock is free, and there is no limit to the number of images, videos, and vectors you can upload for submission. Once you have 30 assets approved, your weekly submission allowance increases based on your approval-to-rejection ratio. To become a Wirestock contributor, follow these simple steps:

- Visit the Wirestock website and click on the 'Sign Up' button in the upper right corner. https://rebrand.ly/wirestock-digitalagemedia
- Fill out the required information and accept the Contributor Agreement.

- Start uploading your photos, vectors, or videos to Wirestock.

Premium Plan and Features

Wirestock offers a premium plan that unlocks additional features for creators. With the premium plan, you get:

- An extra 100 marketplace submissions
- Portfolio Pro access
- Faster keywording and review (completed in less than 48 hours)
- Round-the-clock customer support
- The ability to download files with metadata up to 500GB

Easy Submission Tool

Wirestock's unique "Easy Submission" tool streamlines the submission process by automatically filling out descriptions, titles, and keywords for you. The tool combines the expertise of Wirestock personnel with artificial intelligence (AI) to handle these time-consuming tasks, allowing you to focus on creating great content.

Uploading Photos and Videos

Wirestock offers a versatile and user-friendly platform for creators to upload and sell their visual content online. Supporting multiple upload methods, such as browser, FTP, Google Drive, and Dropbox, Wirestock stands out as one of the few services that accommodate both photo and video submissions. With a range of features designed to provide a seamless experience, Wirestock is an excellent choice for artists and photographers aiming to monetize their work effectively.

Stock Photos

Stock photo websites like Shutterstock (https://www.shutterstock.com/) and iStock (https://www.istockphoto.com/) allow users to download and purchase royalty-free images. With Midjourney, you can create unique and eye-catching digital art to sell on stock photo websites and generate income.

Steps to Sell Art on Stock Photo Websites:

- Sign up for contributor accounts on stock photo websites like Shutterstock and iStock.
- Upload your Midjourney Art to the stock photo websites, following their guidelines and requirements.
- Add relevant keywords and descriptions to your uploaded images to improve searchability.
- Promote your stock photo portfolio on social media and your website to attract potential buyers.
- Monitor your sales and adjust your keywords and descriptions as needed to improve visibility and sales.

Merchandise: Selling Art on Various Products

Merchandise like phone cases, coffee mugs, and tote bags are popular products that people love to purchase. With Midjourney, you can create unique and eye-catching artwork to print on merchandise and sell online. This is a great way to monetize your art and reach a wider audience.

Creating and Selling Art Merchandise:

- Sign up for an account on a print-on-demand platform that offers a variety of merchandise options, such as Redbubble (https://www.redbubble.com/) or Society6 (https://society6.com/).

- Upload your Midjourney Art to the platform and choose the types of products you want to create (e.g., phone cases, coffee mugs, tote bags).

- Adjust your designs to fit the specific product dimensions and requirements.

- Set your pricing and write engaging product descriptions.

- Promote your merchandise store on social media, your website, and other platforms to attract customers and generate sales.

- Monitor your sales and consider creating new designs or adjusting existing ones to keep your store fresh and appealing.

Web Design: Providing Artwork for Web Design Projects

Web designers are always looking for unique and eye-catching artwork to include in their designs. With Midjourney, you can create custom artwork for web designers and charge a fee for your services. This is an excellent way to monetize your art and build a portfolio of work.

Getting Started with Web Design Artwork:

- Create a portfolio website showcasing your Midjourney Art and web design services.
- Network with web designers and agencies by joining online forums, attending industry events, or reaching out directly via email or social media.
- Offer a range of services, from custom illustrations to website background designs, to cater to various client needs.
- Communicate effectively with clients to ensure your artwork aligns with their vision and requirements.
- Deliver high-quality artwork in the required formats and within agreed-upon deadlines.

- Request client testimonials and referrals to help build your reputation and secure more work.

Game Design: Offering Artwork for Video Games

Game designers are continually searching for unique and eye-catching artwork to include in their games. With Midjourney, you can create custom artwork for game designers and charge a fee for your services. This is an excellent way to monetize your art and build a portfolio of work in the gaming industry.

Breaking into the Game Design Industry with Midjourney Art:

- Develop a portfolio website specifically showcasing your Midjourney Art and game design services. Use platforms like Behance (https://www.behance.net/) or ArtStation (https://www.artstation.com/) to create an online portfolio featuring your best work.

- Research game design studios and indie developers to identify potential clients and collaboration opportunities. Studios like Ubisoft (https://www.ubisoft.com/) and indie developers like Supergiant Games (https://www.supergiantgames.com/) are examples of potential clients.

- Network with game designers and developers by joining online forums like Polycount (http://polycount.com/) or TIGForums (https://forums.tigsource.com/), attending industry events like the Game Developers Conference (https://www.gdconf.com/), or reaching out directly via email or social media platforms like LinkedIn or Twitter.
- Offer a range of services, from character design to environment artwork, to cater to various client needs. For example, you could create concept art for characters, design game assets like weapons or vehicles, or develop detailed background environments.

Effective communication with clients is essential for aligning your artwork with their vision and game design requirements. Delivering high-quality artwork in the required formats and within agreed-upon deadlines helps maintain a professional reputation, encouraging repeat business. Building your reputation in the game design industry can be further enhanced by requesting client testimonials and referrals, and showcasing positive feedback on your portfolio website and social media channels. This demonstrates your success and credibility, making you an attractive option for potential clients seeking top-notch artwork for their projects.

By following these steps, you can successfully offer your Midjourney Art for video games and build a thriving business in the gaming industry.

Summary

There are many creative ways to generate income using Midjourney Art. By exploring various platforms and methods, you can monetize your artistic skills and build a successful brand. Remember to be persistent, stay adaptable, and continuously promote your work to reach a wider audience and increase your income potential.

Conclusion

In this book, we've explored the capabilities of Midjourney, demonstrating how to harness it to craft unique and captivating images across a range of styles and industries. From grasping copyright and commercial use concepts to leveraging Chat GPT for constructing effective Midjourney prompts, you now possess the know-how and proficiency to navigate this awesome tool.

We started by exploring the significance of understanding copyright and commercial use while working with Midjourney and managing your subscription. Then, we delved into Discord, helping you get started, comprehend the interface, communicate, and find communities. We also traced the development of Midjourney through its iterations, emphasizing the enhancements and features introduced in each version.

The book equipped you with practical skills for using Midjourney, including adding the bot to your server and employing advanced techniques. We focused on creating efficient prompts and understanding various logo styles and industries, as well as leveraging Chat GPT to generate impressive Midjourney prompts with the assistance of the AIPRM Chrome Extension.

Lastly, we discussed simple methods to generate income using Midjourney art, enabling you to transform your newly acquired skills into a lucrative endeavor.

As you progress, remember to stay informed about the latest advancements in AI and Midjourney by following YouTubers and exploring additional AI tools and resources. Most importantly, have fun and let your creativity flourish as you experiment with Midjourney and Chat GPT.

With a universe of possibilities within reach, you should undoubtedly sign up and start using Chat GPT to elevate your visual creations, if you haven't already. Best of luck on your journey, and enjoy designing!

Recommended YouTubers To Follow For AI

1. Matt Wolfe - https://www.youtube.com/@mreflow
2. Jack Roberts - https://www.youtube.com/@Itssssss_Jack
3. Analog_dreams - https://www.youtube.com/@DreamingInAnalog
4. Sentdex - https://www.youtube.com/user/sentdex
5. Siraj Raval - https://www.youtube.com/channel/UCWN3xxRkmTPmbKwht9FuE5A
6. StatQuest with Josh Starmer - https://www.youtube.com/user/joshstarmer/videos

Useful AI Tools & Other Resources

- AI Tools - https://www.futuretools.io/newly-added
- Apeture by Lexica- https://www.futuretools.io/tools/apeture-by-lexica
- Leonardo.ai - https://futuretools.link/leonardo-ai
- Playground AI - https://futuretools.link/playgroundai
- Dreamlike Studio - https://www.futuretools.io/tools/dreamlike-art
- InstantArt - https://www.futuretools.io/tools/instantart
- BlackBox - https://www.useblackbox.io/signup

One Last Thing

If you've found value from this book or have comments or suggestions, it would be very helpful to others if you would leave an honest review on Amazon. I'd greatly appreciate if you would leave your feedback of this book by scanning the QR code, or by visiting the URL below the QR code.

Post your review on Amazon at this URL:
https://rebrand.ly/midjourney-review

I highly value your input and I personally take the time to read each book review. Your feedback helps me constantly enhance my publications and provide the best possible content for readers.

To be transparent, I would like to address the placement of URLs containing the "rebrandly" prefix throughout the book. This is because I utilize URL shortening and tracking software to more effectively manage multiple URLs and track clicks on the shortened links. By using this software, I am able to analyze website traffic and provide targeted content, which enhances the user experience. Please be assured that the use of this software in no way jeopardizes your privacy or personal information.

If you think the price of failure is too high, the bill from regret will leave you in debt for a lifetime.

Gary Vaynerchuk is one of my favorite people to follow on social media. He speaks very frankly about taking action, has little tolerance for excuses, and encourages taking responsibility, doing what makes **you** happy, and not worrying what **other people** say or think. If you haven't seen any of his videos or content, you should certainly check him out on your choice platform (YouTube, Facebook, Instagram, etc.)—he has insightful and motivating content that many people follow, and I can say that it has helped me along the way when I had doubts.

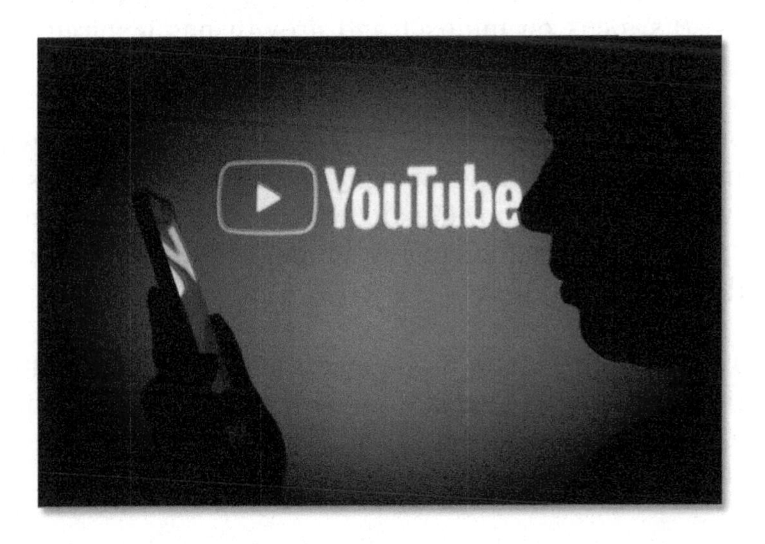

Among the many YouTubers I follow, a few others have had a particularly significant impact on my life as well. Their advice and insights have not only been transformative for me, but can also be life-changing for you if you follow them regularly and implement their guidance.

Graham Stephan, **Meet Kevin**, and **Andrei Jikh** provide practical and entertaining real estate and/or financial advice, which can lead to smarter investment decisions and creating a more secure financial future.

Iman Gadzhi's digital marketing and agency growth tips have been instrumental in helping me navigate the ever-evolving world of online business. But what I appreciate even more about his content is the personal growth insight he shares, which encourages self-discovery and emotional intelligence. Iman's controversial content on topics such as the The Great Reset, and being a Renaissance Man, showcases his intellectual curiosity and diverse range of interests.

Tom Bilyeu's interviews with successful individuals have broadened my perspective and fueled my personal development journey. His focus on mindset and growth has inspired me to continuously learn, adapt, and evolve as a person.

I also hold a deep admiration for the late **Bob Proctor**, whose teachings on personal development and success principles have left a lasting impact on my life. His wisdom and insights continue to inspire countless individuals in their pursuit of personal growth.

Lewis Howes' interviews are among the best I've encountered, featuring engaging conversations with remarkable individuals that leave me feeling motivated and inspired to take action in my own life.

Alex Hormozi is another favorite of mine, as his content on business growth, scaling, and marketing strategies has proven incredibly valuable in shaping my entrepreneurial journey.

By regularly following these YouTubers and others on the list, and implementing their advice, you too can experience a transformation in various aspects of your life. Their collective wisdom can help you achieve your goals, grow your wealth, and unlock your full potential.

I invite you to explore the summaries and use URLs provided for each YouTuber to subscribe to each, as I believe their content can greatly benefit you as well.

- Alex Hormozi - https://www.youtube.com/@AlexHormozi: Business growth expert sharing insights on scaling and marketing strategies for entrepreneurs.

- Andrei Jikh - https://www.youtube.com/@AndreiJikh: Personal finance and investing advice, with a focus on cryptocurrencies and stocks.

- Bedros Keuilian - https://www.youtube.com/@BedrosKeuilian: Fitness business expert providing coaching on sales, marketing, and leadership.

- Biaheza - https://www.youtube.com/@biaheza: E-commerce and dropshipping tutorials, income streams, and business tips.

- Brian Jung - https://www.youtube.com/@Jungernaut: Credit card and personal finance tips, along with investing strategies.

- Cameron Fous - https://www.youtube.com/cameronfous: Stock trading and investment strategies, with a focus on day trading.

- Creative X - https://www.youtube.com/@CreativeXcrew: Digital marketing, e-commerce, and design tips for businesses and creators.

- Ferdy Korpershoek - https://www.youtube.com/@ferdykorpershoek: WordPress tutorials, web design, and online marketing tips.

- GaryVee - https://www.youtube.com/@garyvee: Entrepreneurship, social media marketing, and motivational content.

- Graham Stephan - https://www.youtube.com/@GrahamStephan: Real estate, personal finance, and investing tips.

- Iman Gadzhi - https://www.youtube.com/@ImanGadzhi: Digital marketing and agency growth advice, including social media marketing, personal growth, and financial tips and advice.

- Joshua Mayo - https://www.youtube.com/@JoshuaMayo: Business strategy, digital marketing, and e-commerce tips.

- Kai Andrew - https://www.youtube.com/@KaiAndrew: Entrepreneurship, online business, and marketing strategies.

- Kenan Grace - https://www.youtube.com/@KenanGrace: Stock market news, analysis, and investment tips.

- Lewis Howes - https://www.youtube.com/@lewishowes: Personal development, interviews with successful people, and inspirational content.

- Marc Rebillet - https://www.youtube.com/@MarcRebillet: Live-looping musician and entertainer, known for his improvised performances.

- Mark Tilbury - https://www.youtube.com/@marktilbury : Personal finance, investing, and entrepreneurship advice.

- Matt Wolfe - https://www.youtube.com/@mreflow: Marketing strategies, entrepreneurship, and online business tips.

- Max Maher - https://www.youtube.com/@MaxMaher: Business, finance, and economic news analysis, along with personal finance tips.

- Meet Kevin - https://www.youtube.com/@MeetKevin: Real estate, personal finance, and stock market advice.

- Naam Wynn - https://www.youtube.com/@NaamWynn: E-commerce, dropshipping, and digital marketing tips.

- Nomad Capitalist - https://www.youtube.com/@nomadcapitalist: Global investment strategies, offshore tax planning, and living abroad advice.

- Proctor Gallagher Institute - https://www.youtube.com/@BobProctorTV: Personal development, mindset, and success principles from Bob Proctor.

- Sebastian Ghiorghiu - https://www.youtube.com/@sebb: E-commerce, dropshipping, and online business growth strategies.

- Siraj Raval - https://www.youtube.com/@SirajRaval: Artificial intelligence, machine learning, and data science education.

- Stefanovic - https://youtube.com/@Stefanovic92: Personal finance, investing, and passive income strategies.

- Tatiana James - https://youtube.com/@TatianaJames: E-commerce, Amazon FBA, and online business tips for entrepreneurs.

- Tom Bilyeu - https://www.youtube.com/@TomBilyeu: Personal development, mindset, and interviews with successful individuals in various fields.

I want to thank you again for taking the time to read this book, and I wish you all the best in your future personal and business endeavors.

I hope you enjoyed reading this Digital Age Media book.

To supplement your reading experience and help you implement the strategies outlined in the book, I'll soon be developing a monthly newsletter about AI and I'll also be providing some free PDF downloads with even more tools and resources to help you make the most of the AI tools discussed in this book. Don't let the valuable insights you gained from the book fade in time—sign up for emails to receive special offers, access to bonus content, and info on the latest new releases and other great books from Digital Age Media. On the upcoming website, you'll find blogs and information about AI and other useful information to help you stay informed to achieve even greater success!

YES. Sign me up!

You can scan the QR code or visit the URL below to sign up:
https://rebrand.ly/aibookseries-mini-website

About The Author

A.C. Hamilton is a seasoned entrepreneur, author, and digital marketing expert with over 20 years of experience in the field. Having devoted much of his life to researching and experimenting with effective techniques for earning money locally and online, he has achieved remarkable results thanks to his extensive knowledge and experience.

Determined to share his insights and experiences, A.C. has authored a series of books that equip readers with the tools needed to create sustainable and lasting income. He firmly believes that everyone can achieve economic independence and financial freedom through various digital channels.

A.C. has built an impressive portfolio of enterprises spanning various industries, including real estate, marketing, design, and multiple online businesses, all attributable to his early start in networking and marketing. His debut book, The Firestick Phenomenon, was published on Amazon in 2020, with several new books on topics such as artificial intelligence, LLCs, credit repair, and early success for teenagers set for release throughout 2023.

With a penchant for making people laugh and a positive outlook on life, A.C. brings his upbeat attitude to both business and personal interactions. Beyond his business and literary achievements, he is a classic car enthusiast, golfer, and avid traveler. A.C.'s expertise in entrepreneurship, investing, and family life makes him an invaluable resource for anyone looking to expand their knowledge and achieve success in all aspects of life. Regardless of your experience level, A.C.'s books and digital products offer the tools and guidance needed to thrive.

You can visit A.C.'s author pages on Goodreads and Amazon at the URLs under each image.

rebrand.ly/acgoodreads rebrand.ly/acamazonauthor

You can visit some of A.C.'s other pages at the URLs under each image.

rebrand.ly/bmac

rebrand.ly/ac-linktree

At the link below, you can also sign up to receive emails whenever A.C. Hamilton publishes a new book.

books2read.com/r/B-A-ASRW-RAAHC

Made in the USA
Las Vegas, NV
26 November 2023